Career Quest for Young Professionals

Career Quest for Young Professionals

✦

How to Maintain a Competitive Edge Over Your Peers

Robert T. Uda, MBA, MS, BS²

iUniverse, Inc.
New York Lincoln Shanghai

Career Quest for Young Professionals
How to Maintain a Competitive Edge Over Your Peers

iUniverse books may be ordered through booksellers or by contacting:

iUniverse
2021 Pine Lake Road, Suite 100
Lincoln, NE 68512
www.iuniverse.com
1-800-Authors (1-800-288-4677)

ISBN-13: 978-0-595-40249-6 (pbk)
ISBN-13: 978-0-595-67790-0 (cloth)
ISBN-13: 978-0-595-84625-2 (ebk)
ISBN-10: 0-595-40249-6 (pbk)
ISBN-10: 0-595-67790-8 (cloth)
ISBN-10: 0-595-84625-4 (ebk)

Printed in the United States of America

Career Quest for Young Professionals is dedicated to all of the professional soldiers, sailors, airmen, and marines who serve our country so honorably in Iraq, Afghanistan, and throughout the world. These brave combatants put their lives on the line to protect the freedom of speech that many so-called Americans abuse by tearing down our military men and women. Our military combatants are the real patriots and heroes.

Contents

Preface

*C*areer Quest for Young Professionals provides you with strategies and tactics that you can apply in the workplace to maintain a competitive edge over your peers. It includes principles, secrets, and ideas for achieving significant accomplishments that win you promotions, raises, awards, perquisites, and choice assignments. *Career Quest for Young Professionals* will open eyes, cause outside-of-the-box thinking, and promulgate paradigm shifts.

Career Quest for Young Professionals: How to Maintain a Competitive Edge Over Your Peers works hand-in-hand with four of my other related books. They are as follows:

- *Career Quest for College Graduates: Developing a Successful Career by Leveraging Each of Your Jobs*
- *Career Quest for College Students: Career Development for Those Who Plan to Have a Successful Career*
- *Resumes That Pack a Punch! Creating Beefy Bullets That Grab, Hook, and Wow Hiring Managers into Calling You for an Interview*
- *What Hue Is Your Bungee Cord? Job Searching Strategies for Those Over 40 Years of Age*

If you learn, internalize, and apply the principles enclosed in this book, you will traverse the fast track up your company's organization.

If you disagree with anything that I have written in this book, I encourage you to write me and voice your disagreement. I always like to hear and learn about other people's views on whatever I write. Never do I believe that I know all truth on anything. I am always willing to change my views if someone comes up with contrary responses that make sense to me. That being said, I look forward to hearing from you.

All writings and opinions in this book are solely mine. Any error would be my error only. If you find errors, please bring them to my attention. We will correct them in subsequent editions of this book. I hope you enjoy the real-life stories in this book as I thoroughly have enjoyed living and writing about them. Thank you.

Robert T. Uda
San Marcos, California
June 2006

1

Attitude and Success

Taking a Cue from Fish! *The Fish Philosophy provides an essential element of building effective interpersonal skills. The foundation of the Fish philosophy as proposed by Stephen Lundin and his co-authors in the best selling book, Fish!, is choosing an attitude. This is a daily choice each person makes. A positive attitude and enthusiasm go a long way to developing effective relationships in today's business environment. And only by developing those relationships will managers be able to get things done.*[1]

Particia M. Buhler

O f all the traits to possess to be successful, attitude must be at the top of your list. *Your attitude determines your altitude.* I have never known of any successful person who displayed a negative, pessimistic, bad, destructive attitude. All successful people I know possess positive, optimistic, good, and constructive attitudes. So, start first with a tremendous, fantastic attitude. Maintain an enthusiastic, motivated, positive mental attitude.

> *Your attitude determines your altitude.*

---

1.   Patricia M. Buhler, "Managing in the New Millennium," from *Supervision*: July 2005 issue. As quoted in the March/April 2006 issue of *ICPM Management World* (Harrisonburg, Virginia: Institute of Certified Professional Managers, James Madison University, 2002).

Those Who Succeed

Determination

Here is a statement by an unknown source:

> *"Some succeed because they are destined to, but most succeed because they are determined to."*

It is interesting to note that some of the most naturally talented people in my classes are not determined to succeed. Some with less talent are determined to succeed, and they will succeed because they work harder, do more, overachieve, and are just determined to succeed. These people excite me. They motivate me.

Classes are a Microcosm of Life

The classroom is just a microcosm of what will exist in the companies in which all of you will be working. If you are not determined to be in the top five to six students in the class, you will not be because we do not have students that are destined to succeed in this class.

Those Destined to Succeed

General George S. Patton, Jr., was destined to succeed in World War II. Bill Gates was destined to succeed with Microsoft. Muhammad Ali was destined to succeed as the greatest boxer of all time. Albert Einstein was destined to succeed as a great physicist.

Those Determined to Succeed

I don't see any Pattons, Gates, Alis, or Einsteins in my classes. However, in each class, I do see several people who are *determined to succeed.* Consequently, they will succeed in this class and in their careers after they graduate. This success will result only because they are determined to succeed, for *whatever the mind can conceive and sincerely believe, can be achieved.*

> *Whatever the mind can conceive and believe can be achieved.*

Maximize God-Given Talents

Many students in a class will receive "A's" just by doing the bare minimum. That's fine, because that's all they desire. They don't realize that they are cheating themselves severely by not maximizing their God-given talents to excel if they would just expend the effort to excel.

Do the Best You Can

We don't become "world class" by just doing the bare minimum to get by and receive an "A." We become world class by doing the best we can with what meager talents God has given to us. "*Success is 5 percent inspiration and 95 percent perspiration.*" Anon. Victory is sweet when an average person overcomes disadvantages by climbing into the arena and doing the best he or she can do. That's how they *become the best of the best*. They *never give up or never give in*.

The Person Who Thinks He/She Can

Those with lots of brains and talent squander their blessings by just relegating themselves as "also-rans." That is a crying shame! The race doesn't always go to the swift (remember the tortoise and the hare?) or the crown to the strongest, but it usually goes to the person who thinks he can (remember the little train that made it up and over the mountain because he thought he could?).

> *Success is 5 percent inspiration and 95 percent perspiration.*
> **Anonymous**

Best of the Best

I challenge all students to "*go for it*" during the entire semester. You do not earn your grade unless you give it your all. You do not increase your personal value unless you do your best. I encourage you to be nothing but the best at whatever you do. *Be the best of the best*!

My Dream of "Cream of the Cream"

The Bell Curve Rules

Like everything else in life, everything seems to follow the normal distribution or bell curve. There are a few who love my World Wide Web Course Tools (WebCT) course website; there are a whole bunch in a class who think it is okay; and there are those who think it is terrible. The distribution of the class is the same going from

> *Be the best of the best!*

one semester to the next when my Microsoft FrontPage website was only one-tenth as good as the WebCT one. The same normal distribution of opinions of the website existed then. So, it seems that no matter what I do, some people will complain about whatever condition (good, bad, or indifferent) that exists.

Beggars Should Not Be Choosers

If I gave people a hot, sizzling, grilled filet mignon on a silver platter at no charge to them, there will be a few who will complain about it. You know the usual complaints: It's too raw. It's too well done. It has no seasoning. It's too late; we had to wait too long for it. It is too tough. It tastes terrible. And on and on it goes. You know, it is the usual mantra. They fail to realize that "beggars should not be choosers."

Silver Lining in Every Dark Cloud

I think, though, complaining is just an outlet for people. If they aren't griping about something, they wouldn't be happy. This is why I like to associate only with positive, constructive, enthusiastic people. Too many people see a half-filled glass of water as being half empty instead of half full. Half full is the way both you and I should like to look at things. There is always a silver lining in every dark cloud. My wife always sees the good in everything and everyone. That is why she is so good for me.

Don't Be Satisfied with Mediocrity

Little do these complainers know, however, is that the attitudes that they have in college will be maintained throughout their lives. Then, they will wonder why they don't receive all of the goodies that a few people always seem to get on the job and in life in general. Unless they catch themselves and initiate a paradigm shift, they will be just the typical run-of-the-mill workers throughout their careers and lives. However, if they are happy with doing and being that way, then, for them, it is good. But for the few of us go-getters, we are not satisfied with mediocrity and just being an also-ran, for we cannot and will not tolerate such behavior. So, I guess that is good that they are that way…they provide less competition for those of us who expect the best and get it.

Weeding Out the Slackers

I have found that in every class that I have taught, there are about one-to-three students who hate my guts. No matter what I do, they cannot and will not be appeased. I wonder why they take the course. It is an elective for goodness sakes! Why do they make life unbearable for themselves and for me? That's why I had attempted to weed out the "slackers" at the beginning of the semester. These are the students who will write nasty things about me on their evaluations at the end of the semester. They will complain about me behind my back to my supervisor and the administration. They will badmouth me to other students and people.

With Such Friends, Who Needs Enemies?

I hope these people don't expect all of the goodies in their careers. The way they go about attempting to ruin other people's careers, they will have the same things happening to them in their careers. These are the people that cannot be trusted. They will be the people who will work in companies like Enron, WorldCom, GlobalCrossing, and Tyco. With friends like that, who needs enemies?

Dual Responsibility in the Learning Process

At any rate, I really appreciate students who feel that they also have an obligation in the learning process. Too many of them sit there and expect the instructor to pour knowledge into their brains. They do not realize that, for good learning to occur, they need to carry their part of the responsibility.

Student Responsibilities in the Learning Process

Students need to buy the book (some do not buy the required textbook!). Students need to read the assigned materials. Students need to review the course website. Students need to read their emails on a daily basis and no less than once a week (I wonder if some of our students ever think about looking at their emails daily?). Students need to do the assignments and turn them in either early or on time, not late as some do. Students need to follow the "guidelines" and other instructions. Students need to listen to the lectures and guest speakers and participate in the discussions. Students need to be at every class and not cut class in a willy-nilly fashion. Students need to have a desire for learning and to question things. Questioning is not equal to griping. Students need to study for the quizzes and the mid-term exam. I wonder if a handful of our students ever realize that they have these responsibilities?

Instructor's Responsibilities

I'm fulfilling my responsibility by working 10–16 hours a day on trying to prepare for and to make the course better than the previous semester. I read my emails on the average of every 30 minutes every day. I'm constantly reading new materials appearing on the various websites so that I can bring the latest information to my students either in email attachments or additions to the website. However, when I do that, I get complaints that there is too much information provided. Last semester, some students complained about receiving too many emails. So, I cut down on doing that in the present semester. Yet, I still receive complaints of too much information being provided on the course website.

Why are Students in College?

Sometimes I wonder for what some students are in college. Are they here just to get an "A"…whether they learn anything or not? I would rather have a "B" student who learns a lot and applies that knowledge in his/her career than an "A" student who didn't learn a thing and wasted his/her (and my) time in this class. Why do students take this elective course if they feel they are going to learn nothing from the get-go? That attitude baffles me for someone earning a degree in business. This is one reason why I prefer to teach graduate students. We don't have as much of that negativism with which to deal.

Cream de Cream

So, in winding down this soapbox discussion, I just want to say that I do love positive students and love to teach great and wonderful things. I wish I could teach classes with only the "cream of the crop." I'll take the half-dozen or so of the top students (not necessarily "A" students) in each of my classes over the past four semesters and make them even better performers than they are currently. These will be the titans of the business world and industry after they graduate. In my opinion, if we had nothing but "go-getters" in the class, it would be nirvana or a near utopia for me. Every student would be feeding off the positiveness of all of the other students. All would be edified and motivated, would strive harder, and would become even better. That is my dream in life…to teach nothing but the *Einsteins*.

Go for It!

Be Positive and Confident in Yourselves

I want students to think, reason, evaluate, come to conclusions, make decisions, and just display some wisdom at such a young age. I want all of you to be positive and confident in yourselves. I want you to pursue your passion. I want you to *"think outside of the box."* I want you to *"get outside of your comfort zone"* and to *"push the envelope."* I want you to write bullets and resumes that *"pack a punch."* I want you to get the best jobs you can.

Seize the Day!

Don't worry about the future. Just set your goals and prepare a plan. Implement your plan. Compete for the gold. Be world class or the best of the best. *Expect the best and get it.* So, pursue your passion. Take up photography. Write that book. Remember, when you write/publish a book, you will become an instant authority on whatever you write. You will gain instant credibility. So, self-actualize. Be a mover and shaker. Make things happen. Do it now! Don't let grass grow under your feet. *Seize the day!*

Make Your Mark on the World

Go out there and make your mark on the world. Be creative and innovative in all you do. You will be a big success in life. Don't let anyone make you believe otherwise. Luck to you always!

Your Attitude Determines Your Altitude

An Observation

The Loser's Limp

Have you ever noticed that sprinters practice their start and work to get it down to a science? The sprinter who gets off a step ahead of his competitors most likely wins the 100-meter dash. Why is that? Well, when you get ahead of the bunch with a good start, you psych out the others and put a slight doubt in their minds. Those who fall behind give up and don't even try to win the race. They display the loser's limp.

Get Off to a Good Start

It is no different in going after the awards in class or going after points in the course. Those who get ahead from the beginning stay at the front of the pack. Those who have a slow start always seem to be at the bottom of the various totems. Hence, it is important to get an "edge" over your competitors by starting-off with a bang and maintaining a fast pace throughout the race. This is the time to *increase your stride and accelerate your pace.*

Compete for the Goodies

If you don't go after the points and you don't go after the awards (as small as they may seem), you forfeit yourself from receiving the goodies in class and later receiving the goodies in the companies for which you work. If you don't compete in class, you won't compete in your future companies. Don't fall into the paradigm that you will just do a good, steady job and then expect to win any of the goodies.

> *Increase your stride and accelerate your pace.*

That won't happen unless you were in a communistic organization where they detest competition.

Overachieve to Win

Those who go after points and awards are usually the hardest workers, produce the most work, and create the best quality work. This is because they have a winning attitude. There is nothing worse than not going all out when you possess the most talents of everyone else around. However, I've observed that those who win are usually those without the most talents. They use that lack of talent to motivate themselves to try harder, run faster, run longer, prepare more, work longer, work harder, and work smarter than everyone else around them.

Don't Ever Settle for Second Best

So, friends, the race isn't over yet, unless (in the recesses of your mind) you do believe it is over. *Whatever the mind can conceive and sincerely believe can be achieved. Don't ever settle for second best. Expect the best and get it!*

Expect the Best and Get It!

Strive to Do Your Best

I love it when people (students included) always strive for the top slot in everything and anything they pursue. What I cannot understand is why some students take my course if they won't bother to expend even a meager effort. That's why I wanted to weed out the "slackers" at the beginning of the course. It irritates me to no end when I see students who won't even try to do their best. What are they doing getting a degree in business for anyway?

Compete to Become the Best

Business life is based on competition, free and open markets, supply and demand, survival of the fittest, capitalism, and striving for success. If students don't want to be involved in these things, why are they in business in the first place? They ought to get into career fields such as art, music, philosophy, history, and other such majors. Even then, they should compete. Why become an artist if you don't want to become the best artist in the world? Why become a vocalist or musician if you won't strive to become a world-class vocalist or musician? Even if I was going to be a garbage man, I would want to become the best garbage man in the world!

Don't Be a Slacker

Slackers will be a drain on the companies for which they work. They will just be punching a timecard and putting in their eight hours a day. They will be money spenders instead of money makers in the company. They won't make an effort to earn promotions and raises, yet they expect to get these things, which are set aside only for those who go "above and beyond" what's expected on the job description. That's why some students cannot write good bullets. They need to do something spectacular first before they can write about it.

Paradigm Shift Needed

I hope that those who are not making any effort to be number one and to win awards available for all to pursue will initiate a paradigm shift today, get off their duffs, and start doing something. I work day and night, weekends, and holidays to prepare information to spoon feed important principles/strategies of my course to all class members. Further, some keep their mouths closed and not learn any of the information to help them capture a good job and thereafter perform well on the job.

Why are You in the Business Administration Degree Program?

If they don't want a good job, what are they pursuing a college degree anyway! However, I think they really want a good job but will do the bare minimum to get a good job. Fat chance for them! That will never happen unless their dad owns the company. The important question is this: If anyone doesn't want to get a good paying job that they love, then for what are they in college? Looking for a spouse? Nothing better to do? Because everyone else is doing it? Trying to find themselves? Because their parents are footing the bill? All of these are not good reasons for being in the business administration degree program.

Avoid Mediocrity Like the Plague

Well, I've soap boxed enough. I just get really irritated when I see students with so much talent as all of my students in my classes have, yet some won't exploit their talents to hone their skills and become the best that they can be. Mediocrity is sinful and should be avoided like the plague. Only those who "expect the best and get it" are those whom I want in my classes.

Shortcomings Can Become Your Motivators

I would like to tell you that I admire your commitment and motivation to continue. It is a real inspiration to know when you had mentioned that you had a low GPA when you got your first bachelor's degree. However, that did not matter, and you continued ahead. Thank you for motivating others (i.e., me). It seems that I needed to hear your story to truly start believing in myself (a little embarrassing to be unconfident because I am a middle-aged person). Just a thought.

Use Setbacks as Motivators

Throughout my life, I have had many shortcomings and disadvantaged. However, I used those setbacks as the motivators to try harder (mostly fear motivation), not giving up, and doing more than everyone else around me.

Handicaps and Inferiority Complexes Motivated Me

When I was in high school, I never believed I could graduate from college. I felt I was really dumb! Yet, the funny thing is that others around me thought I was smart. I stuttered and stammered for the first 20–25 years of my life. I was a true, shy introvert. I had numerous inferiority complexes about my looks, myself, my capabilities, and my self-concept. However, all of these handicaps and inferiority complexes motivated me to prove myself to others and to the world instead of giving up…as many people do. Hence, I tried harder, did more, competed, and never gave up or gave in. Everyone can do likewise.

Always Make a Try for It

It is better to try and fail than to have never tried at all. If you never try for anything, you will always wonder if you could have done it. That's not a good way to go through life.

Gradual Uphill Process, Not a Step Function

Yes, winning an award is just a small thing. However, triumphing on big things always starts with small triumphs. I don't know of anybody who started as a nobody with talent who became world class the next day on the first try. *From little acorns do gargantuan oak trees grow!* But it is always a gradual, uphill process, not a step function.

Don't Give Up or Give In

Don't ever let your age hold you back. You can do wonders for the rest of your life. I'm finally going to start on a doctorate program this year, and I'm 63 going on 64 years of age! Most people are retiring when I'm planning on starting a new career. So, don't give up or give in. You can do great and wonderful things if you think you can, for whatever the mind can conceive and sincerely believe can be achieved. Your attitude determines your altitude. Onward and upward!

2

Creativity, Innovation, and Patience

With routine tasks being increasingly automated and the competitive environment becoming more dynamic, creative problem solving and innovation will play a greater role in determining future managers' success or failure. **Creativity** *is the process of generating new and useful ideas.* **Innovation**, *on the other hand, is taking a new idea and putting it to use. Managers can increase their subordinates' creativity through the climate they create and the way they treat their subordinates. The implementation of creative ideas (i.e., innovating) must overcome people's resistance to change.*[2]

Dr. Scott Williams
Wright State University

I f you really want to make a significant impact on your job and in your life, you must develop the ability to be creative and innovative. You must discover something, invent something, change things, improve things, and develop things. Have you had an original thought yet today? You must come up with original thoughts on a daily basis.

Be impatient about it. Make everything urgent. Do it now! Never let grass grow under your feet. Do things immediately if not sooner. Make things happen. Be a doer. Be a mover and a shaker. Upset the apple cart. Make a difference and make the world a better place because you lived in it.

---

2. Dr. Scott Williams, "Leading Creativity and Innovation," *The LeaderLetter*, Department of Management, Raj Soin College of Business, Wright State University, Dayton, Ohio. Extracted on 5/29/06 from the following URL: http://www.wright.edu/~scott.williams/LeaderLetter/innovation.htm#Transformational%20Leadership—Converting%20Creative.

Firms Seeking People Who are Ahead of Their Time

Can you recommend any marketing firms or types of marketing firms that accept cutting-edge, unique people and uncommon ideas?—Darren Garrow

I cannot recommend specific marketing firms by name (with one exception below). However, I can recommend the types of marketing firms that accept cutting-edge, unique people, and uncommon ideas.

Work for Creative Companies

If you want to work in a huge corporation that epitomizes creativity and innovation, look at companies like Walt Disney. You can also look at the major toy companies (go to "Ask Jeeves" at http://www.ask.com). However, if you really want to get in with the creative bunch, you should look at small firms or new startups with great, cutting-edge products. For example, many video game companies create new, exciting games every day. I have a friend who designs complex, classy video games.

Associate with Entrepreneurs

You should look for the entrepreneurs (like yourself) who seek exciting things to do because of their low boredom thresholds. Go to "Ask Jeeves" and punch in *inventors, creative people, innovators,* and other such similar words. You will see many individuals and small firms that you could investigate.

Categories of Creative, Innovative People

Creative, innovative people come in many categories such as the following:

- Researchers, discoverers, experimenters
- Creators, inventors, patentees, conceptualizers
- Creative writers, authors, poets, novelists
- Musicians, vocalists, songwriters, entertainers (including athletes), hosts
- Artists, sculptors, painters, model makers, crafters
- Thespians/actors playwrights, comedians, movie makers, scriptwriters, producers
- Computer programmers, multi-media experts
- Designers, creators, architects, mathematicians, scientists, engineers, technologists, consultants, teachers
- Innovators, idea people, dreamers, geniuses, marketers, philosophers, big-picture folks

- Stylists, color coordinators, events coordinators
- Leaders, managers, executives, politicians, charismatic individuals, orators, military strategists, pied pipers
- Travelers, adventurers, discoverers, thrill seekers
- Entrepreneurs, organizers, promoters, planners, builders
- Champions of all categories, world-class individuals, those who are "best of the best"
- Value adders, movers and shakers, doers, those who make things happen

Associate with Creative, Innovative People

Most creative, innovative people are right-brained people. However, there are left-brained people who can also be creative and innovative. Usually, it doesn't come as natural to left-brained people as it does to right-brained people. Find these kinds of creative/innovative people and get to know them. Associate with these kinds of people. Many of them can develop ingenious products, but they don't know how to commercialize and market their ideas and products. This is where you come in.

Start Your Own Creative Business

If you cannot find any such firms, start your own firm and promote your own cutting-edge, unique personality and uncommon ideas. Find others like yourself and create either products or ideas for marketing these ingenious products. Become a consultant to all of these geniuses out there who develop great products but who don't know how to market them. There is more than one way to skin a cat!

Creating a New Job

I have been thinking about presenting upper management in my company with a new position for myself. The position would be a recruiter type position where I would go to schools, job fairs, etc., explaining the options my company offers. How should I go about presenting this idea to my Director of Education? What meeting type should I use, i.e., lunch, in person, over the phone, etc.? When should I present them with this idea if I will not be graduating until May 2006? What do I base my expected pay on if it is not an established position in this company, and I have little experience?— Nicole Seguine

That's a Good Idea!

That's a good idea! Prepare a PowerPoint (PP) presentation using effective graphics and color. Set up a meeting with your director of education to give this PP presentation to him in person in a conference room. Start this project as soon as possible…the sooner the better.

Base your expected pay on where Kim Martin of Enterprise started. Perhaps you could contact her and tell her what you are planning to do. She may be in a better position to give you at least a range of what your proposed starting salary should be. Actually, you will be doing exactly what Kim Martin of Enterprise is doing as well as what Emlyn Wyman of Hertz is doing. They are both recruiters for their respective companies. You would be a great recruiter!

Do It Now!

Even if the director of education does not accept your proposal, it will indicate to him that you have shown initiative, which is a desirable quality. If something similar presents itself in his department, your name would certainly be stored in the recesses of his memory. Consequently, you may be the first one he would seek to fill such a position. So, no matter what happens, you will benefit. The exercise will also be good experience for you. Remember, the worst that can happen is that he would reject your idea. He won't kill you. Who knows? He may think it is a fabulous idea and implement it immediately. I say, do it now!

Patience

Accelerating the Process to Become a Personal Banker

After six months of working with Bank of America as a teller, I have been doing what a personal banker does with the same salary and position. My manager really appreciates what I am doing and tells me to keep up with my hard work. My manager has been telling me since two months ago that she is going to send me to school to become a personal banker. Last week, I talked to my manager and she told me to wait because the bank was cutting hours. Is there anything I can do to accelerate the process of becoming a personal banker?—Omar Garcia-Machado

Patience is a Virtue

Unless things change and business increases, Bank of America will continually postpone your going to school to become a personal banker. One way to accelerate the process of becoming a personal banker is to seek work simultaneously at several other banks. You must let them know of your strong desire to become a personal banker, so they will hire you to go directly to school to become a personal banker. Other than that, you just need to be patient and wait for Bank of America to act in your favor.

Make Things Happen

I was never patient when I was your age. Hence, I always seem to characterize the cartoon of a couple of vultures sitting on a tree limb. One turns to the other saying, "Patience, heck (the more color word meaning Hades was used), I'm going to kill something!" In other words, rather than wait for the next foot to drop, I proactively did things to make things happen sooner rather than later. I was not successful in every case; however, in most cases, I made things happen one way or another.

Can You Handle the Risk?

Hence, it is up to you as to whether you want to stay with Bank of America for a long time or be like that vulture and go kill something. The risk of taking my approach is that I never stayed with one company for a very long time. Though, I did remain in the USAF for over eight years and worked for Rockwell International for seven years. However, most of the other companies I worked for ranged anywhere from one to three years. That's why I worked for a dozen companies during a 40-year career.

Bird in Hand or Two in the Bush?

I just got a job offer with Bank of America (BOA) as a teller today. I also interviewed with Washington Mutual (WaMu) last Tuesday. They said to call back on Friday, so I did, and I was told that they had an interview scheduled on Tuesday (yesterday). They said they did not call back because they were still interviewing and not to think that they didn't like me. I called back this morning, and I talked to the manager who said that there were more interviews; I think they just were sent more applicants. She said to hang in there and that she would personally call me back when a job offer is ready. It sounded like I would get the offer, but now, I'm not sure. I believe WaMu pays better because I have a friend who works there and the offer from BOA is less than what they got. How long should I wait for get a job offer from WaMu? I told Bank of America that I could respond by Friday or next Monday.—Steven Tran

Good Negotiating Position

You are in a good negotiating position. You currently have the BOA job offer in hand, which you had received today. WaMu is presently toying with you. All they are doing is looking for a better candidate to give an offer to by continuing to interview other job applicants. You need to force their hand. Tell them that you "really" want to come to work for them; however, you have an offer in-hand from BOA and that you need to give them their decision by Monday. This may shake loose an offer from WaMu.

Negotiating is a Game of Perception

By the way, did you tell BOA that you had a pending offer from WaMu? If you did not, you should. That gets them quite nervous. They may even increase their offer to you when they realize that they may lose you. By leveraging one against the other, that is how your personal stock increases in value in the minds of both hiring managers. *Negotiating the best offer is all a game of perception.* If they perceive you of higher value, they would offer you a sweeter deal.

> *Negotiating the best offer is all a game of perception.*

Don't Burn Your Bridges

When Monday arrives and if you have not received an offer from WaMu, accept the BOA offer. Then, if WaMu comes through with their offer, say for example, next Wednesday, negotiate and accept that offer. Then, go back to BOA and sadly tell them that the WaMu offer had come through and that you had accepted their offer, so you now need to withdraw your acceptance of the BOA offer. Be nice about it. In other words, do not "burn your bridges."

You could also make an acceptance after you start working for a couple of weeks with BOA. I have seen that happen before when I had worked at HR Textron, Inc. A new employee there quit after a couple of weeks on the job to accept a better deal. He left on good terms.

Thank You Card, Note, or Email

Because I have had bad experiences with BOA in the past, I am not very high on BOA. On the other hand, since my daughter, Heather, was treated very well by WaMu and is now back working for them, naturally, I am partial to WaMu and feel it is a better bank. Perception is everything. Hence, if you feel the same way about WaMu, then you need to try to "pull" an offer from the WaMu hiring manager. I hope you had sent the WaMu hiring manager a thank you card, note, or email. If you did, great! If you didn't, shame on you. Do it now!

3

Finding Yourself

Want to know a way to figure out whether your current career path is the right one? Get to know yourself a little bit better. It's hard enough finding jobs these days, but finding a job that is as enjoyable as it is personally rewarding can be a hard balance to achieve. Perhaps it's time to look within for the answers.[3]

Staff Writer
The Career News

Many people are lost. They don't know what they want to do when they grow up. What a predicament to be in particularly if they are graduating from college. They should never fear. Life will go on. They should try different things to find out where their life interests will lead them. It's okay to fail. Learn from every failure. That way, when you succeed, you will appreciate the success immensely. Go forward with faith!

What to Do if You Find Your Interests Have Changed

If after I work for a couple years, I realize I despise my job and/or industry, what do I do then? I think this is a fear that many college students have. Many of us go to college because it is what we are supposed to do, but we do not know what we want to do or what it is like once we get into the real world. Once we get enough into a major to realize we might not like it, it's too late unless we want to incur additional loans and expenses.

---

3. Staff Writer, "Identify your perfect career—free test," *The Career News*, May 9, 2005, issue, Vol. 5, Issue 18.

What! Me Worry?

The gist of the entire answer is "Don't worry about it." Follow *Mad Magazine*'s Alfred E. Newman's motto: "What! Me worry?" Your career will cover three to six different career fields/jobs throughout the next four or more decades. So, enjoy the journey. Go with the flow. You should be constantly going to school and acquiring lifelong learning anyway. Be flexible. Follow your passion or passions. Always know that, whatever choice you make, it will be the correct choice for you at that moment in time.

Find Your Niche in Life

Hence, after you work for a couple of years and find that you despise your job and/or industry, just look for another job in another industry. So what? There's no skin off your nose. Just go on to the next mountain (challenge) and scale that mountain too. Then, when you get tired of that mountain, go on to the next one. Don't ever look at it as failures. Look at it as another attempt at finding your niche in life. Look at it as just another quest to find your true passion. There's nothing wrong with that!

You Have No Need to Fear

There is no need to fear. President Franklin Delano Roosevelt said, "The only thing to fear is fear itself." *Remember this: If you are prepared for whatever is coming down the pike, you have no need to fear.* Most of it is an attitude, for your attitude determines your altitude. If you are prepared for surprises, you have no need to fear. If you are flexible, you have no need to fear. If you see a glass half full instead of half empty, you have no need to fear. If you have supreme confidence in yourself and your abilities, you have no need to fear.

> *If you are prepared for whatever is coming down the pike, you have no need to fear.*

Having Fun is a State of Mind

Remember, no matter what direction you are headed, it is never too late. My career has been a real roller-coaster ride. But it has been sheer, exhilarating fun all along the tracks. It has been fun only because I made up my mind that it was going to be fun. There is no room for unhappiness. I have no regrets.

Concerned About Taking the Wrong Path?

However, what if I make or take the wrong path? One of our in-class speakers said, "Don't be afraid to leave a job you hate," but what if you like it and see a very prosperous future in the job? What do you do? Then, on the other hand, do I really need to have my whole life planned out at 23 years old?

Plan Ahead to Get Ahead

If you like your job, keep it. Only if you hate your job should you consider leaving it for something better. As I said before, do not worry about taking the wrong path. You can always change your direction if you find you had made a mistake. No, you do not really need to have your entire life planned out at the age of 23. However, those that do plan their lives are miles ahead of those who do not.

Planning to Become a Nobel Prize Winner

I remember reading a magazine article years ago about a medical research doctor who kept a detailed record of every article, paper, and document that he had read in the area of his research by title, author, name of magazine/journal it was in, date, number of pages, etc. He planned to read a certain number of pages each day. He kept meticulous records of everything he did. All of this was for the overall goal of winning the Nobel Prize for Medicine. Can you believe that! This doctor had planned his life by the hour to become a Nobel Prize Winner years from that point in life. I do not know if he made it or not, but that article made quite an impression on me when I read it.

Without Goals, Nowhere is Your Destination

Those who plan their lives ahead are usually those who accomplish great things. If you do not have a goal and a plan to accomplish that goal, chances are, you will never achieve that goal. I do not know of any winners who had accomplishments just fall into their laps without any expended effort. If you have no goal, any path will get you there, which is nowhere.

I Have No Idea What I Should Do After Graduating

I have been a manager for a retail company for five years. I now have concluded that I hate retail, but I love managing. For so long, I always hoped to get into a corporate position with a large retail company. However, I have no corporate experience, and I'm afraid that most companies want someone with more experience or at least working in that company for so many years. I definitely do NOT want to work for the company I am in now due to the large corporate turnover.

When I graduate in a year, I also have an account manager job waiting for me. However, I am not sure if I want to sit in an office every day of my life. I don't know what I should do after graduating. I know I love managing people, but I don't want to be in a store as a manager. Do you have any insights or suggestions on what I should do after I graduate?

Working in the Corporate Office

One thing I know for sure. You cannot start at the corporate office without first gaining experience at the lower working levels of the company unless, of course, you took a secretarial or administrative assistant job at the corporate office. To get into the corporate office as a manager on your first real job after graduating from college, you need to be well connected with the CEO to achieve such an opportunity. If you don't have any such connections, then forget about that pipe dream until you gain a few years of solid experience under your belt at the lower levels.

Account Manager Position

Don't slough off the account manager job you already have waiting for you. It does have the word "manager" in the title. You didn't explain the duties of that account manager position, so I cannot comment on it. However, the many account manager positions I have been exposed to are outside sales and/or marketing jobs. They go out to meet customers and "press the flesh" so to speak. They develop products, participate in pricing, get involved in promoting the products, and land large contracts from clients. They spend much of their time "on the road" as opposed to sitting in an office every day.

Management Positions Everywhere

There are more management positions than those just in the retail industry. There are a myriad of industries that you can consider such as wireless communications, biotechnology, pharmaceutical, aerospace, defense, gaming, computers, food, transportation (bus, train, air travel, shipping (air/sea freight, overnight express mail, and trucking), auto rental, and cruise ships), entertainment, tourism, real estate, and construction. You can be a manager in any of those industries just as well as you can in the retail clothing industry. So, broaden your horizons and investigate management positions in many of these other industries that may strike your fancy.

Find Your Passion

Find your passion and then get a job that accommodates your passion. Try different kinds of jobs. When you find where you want to spend your entire career, then work your way into management. Managing people is fun, but after a while, you may find (as I did) that it's not all cracked up to be what it seems. Hence, you need to get into management quickly so you will either excel in it or purge it from your system and then pursue what really makes you happy.

Is Business the Right Career Field for Me?

After these last few sessions of class and listening to our guest speakers, all this talk about finding a career that is right for you, one that will make you happy, and one that you like and look forward to every day has me perplexed. After listening to my peers and talking to them, I've really been asking myself the question: "What do I want to do with the rest of my life?"

Lately, especially after hearing my peers argue about Senior Experience, the whole issue of how some groups took the initiative to get what they wanted by being aggressive and seeking the desired topics has got me really thinking. Our guest speakers talk about how it is important to be aggressive to get what you want in the business world. Hence, I am beginning to doubt whether I chose the right major. I am not sure if the business world is right for me.

I guess, maybe, after I get more work experience, I will feel differently about it. I just feel like I am not going to fit into the aggressive business world because I feel like I am not aggressive enough. What I am asking is this: "How do I know if I will fit into the business world?" How do I know I will not fail in the business world?

Why You are Perplexed

Upon looking at your Career Success Map Questionnaire (CSMQ) and Jung Typology Test (JTT) or Myers-Briggs Type Indicator (MBTI) results, it is apparent why you are perplexed. In your CSMQ, you scored a 12 under "Getting Balanced," and 12 is the strongest intensity level for this orientation. That means you strongly desire a meaningful balance between work, important relationships, and personal development. You also strongly focus on flexibility and efficiency.

What You Really Desire

From that information, it is apparent that you do not desire to be aggressive, to be the queen of the mountain, and/or to be keenly competitive or combative. Instead, you desire to work only to provide a sufficient income for your happy family. You are more concerned about relationships and getting along rather than aggressively competing and beating your competitors. Additionally, you strongly desire to grow, develop, and enjoy life personally instead of being involved with political hassles in the workplace. You desire peace, compromise, and happiness over confrontation, winner takes all, anger, hatred, and other such negative emotions prevalent in the corporate jungle.

What You Really Want to Be

Now, looking at your JTT/MBTI information, you are an ISFJ introvert. That further corroborates your high score of "Getting Balanced" on your CSMQ. An ISFJ person is one who is introverted sensing with feeling. That is you! You are service and work oriented. You like to serve others and be a worker bee rather than a leader, executive, or queen bee. Because you are a hard worker, you may suffer from tiredness, exhaustion, and fatigue. A caution is that you may be attracted to troublemakers. Although, I hope that is not true for you. At any rate, avoid them.

Jobs You Would Be Good at Doing

Some of the jobs that you would be good at doing include the following:

- Nurse
- School teacher
- Secretary
- Medical doctor (general practitioner type)
- Librarian
- Middle manager
- Housekeeper

You have a personality like Laura Bush, who was a librarian before she married President George W. Bush.

Your Fit Into These Jobs

Take a close look at those seven jobs listed above. As you would need to be aggressive in the business world, every listed job above requires you to be a non-aggressive competitor. All of those jobs are service-oriented jobs. The nurse and doctor help sick and injured patients get well. The schoolteacher and librarian help children and students learn good things. The secretary helps her boss become successful at whatever he does. The housekeeper helps clients maintain a clean and efficient household. Should you remain in the business milieu, even the middle manager services her bosses, works closely with peers (i.e., other middle managers), and services subordinates/direct reports in doing their work.

You are a Doer, Not a Talker

It is clear that you are not the type to be in competition with others for position, power, and fame. You do not want to be nor will you ever rise to be a chief executive officer (CEO). You are not the type to order others to do things. You are more of a team player, staff person, and/or a supportive person. You are a doer, not a talker. Can you see why you are perplexed about the highly competitive business world?

What You Could Do

Once you receive your BSBA degree, you could go into nursing, teaching, library science, or medicine. If you remained in business, you could get into business administration in the services sector. For example, you could go into human resources. That would use your business degree, yet you would be working with people. You could get into marketing/sales, finance/accounting, purchasing, and/or contract administration. You could go into selling insurance, claims adjusting, recruiting, public relations, events planning, research, and/or charity work. Therefore, you can do a wide array of things as a career.

Stay the Course

Just remember this: Find your passion and be the best in the world at it. By doing that, you will be extremely happy no matter what field or vocation you pursue. A business degree gives you a good, solid foundation for almost any field you go into (with the exception of highly technical (e.g., engineering, science, and technology) or specialized fields (medicine, law, airline pilot, and air traffic controller), so do not get discouraged about being in the business school.

A business degree teaches you leadership, management, administration, accounting and finance, marketing, group interaction, researching, writing, public speaking, human resources, international marketing/management, business law, and economics. All of these are useful and good to know no matter what occupation you pursue in the future. So, for the present, stay the course.

What Should I Do?

Everything was supposed to go according to plan. My plan was that I was going to graduate in the fall of 2006 and continue working in my current job (I currently am working for a small business owner in the insurance industry. I have been working for him for almost 2½ years.). I enjoy almost every aspect of my job from the customers to the pay.

While in school, I am currently working only about 25 hours a week. However, as of January 2006, I will be working more on a full-time basis. My plan has always been to have a full-time job offer after I graduate from college. Amazingly, this has happen. My boss has offered me a full-time job with unlimited potential. My starting salary could be anywhere from $45K, plus commission and bonuses, with the possibility to take over his business when he retires. How perfectly planned-out could my plan get, right? Wrong!

For a couple months now, I have been contemplating my career path. I had always planned to stay in my current job but have been starting to question if this is what I really want to do. This class has really opened my eyes and made me question many things. One is this: Can I do my current job for the next 35 years of my life? The answer to that is, yes. On the other hand, can I do it for the next five years of my life? The answer to this question is: I don't know.

Recently, I have started to think of all the other possibilities there are, both when it comes to my career and in life. For example, should I move to a different state, possibly Florida, for the next couple of years with the intention of experiencing new things in life, while trying to figure out what I want to do in life, or should I change career path completely? I am really stuck at a fork in the road when it comes to my life's path. What should I do to determine what path I should take?

When You Come to a Fork In the Road, Take It!

As Yogi Berra says, "When you come to a fork in the road, take it!" In other words, don't worry about which fork you take, just take one. You are worrying too much about what path you should take and compounding it by worrying about it should you make a mistake. So what if you make a mistake! If things don't go right with one path, take another path and go with it.

Enjoy the Trips!

The first thing I suggest to you is to find out what you are most passionate about. Next, find the jobs that would meet that passion. Then, get one of those jobs and go for it! Enjoy the journey. If after a few years, you find that it is not fun any more, grab the next job you are passionate about and go for it! Keep doing that process until you find your real passion in life. In the meantime, enjoy the trips!

Where am I Going with My Life?

You and your class have really got me thinking about what I want to be when I grow up! I mean I know that I am pursuing and accomplishing all these goals toward being an administrator of a retirement home some day, which is something for which I truly have a passion.

However, I am having difficulties staying on track because of my question that I stated in the beginning. What do I want to be when I grow up? To help people, I remember always wanting to be some type of doctor such as a physical therapist, child therapist, or even hotel and restaurant management.

I even had plans to attend Northern Arizona University. But then, of course, things changed when I became pregnant at such a young age and had no choice but to keep going to school and to find a job quickly. Don't get me wrong; I am very happy with where I am in my life.

The struggle is "Where am I going with my life?" Do you just come to a point where you are getting too old for all the dreams you wanted and you just have to make a decision because time is of the essence? Or is there any way to be more than one thing? Is this what turns into consulting work, or am I on the wrong page? Your guidance is appreciated greatly.

Follow Your Passions

Whatever you do regarding your career choices, follow your passion or passions. If you do that, you will never go wrong and will always be happy in your career. You may end up have anywhere between three and six career changes throughout your working lifetime. In my 40-year career thus far, I have worked through 10 different career fields and 7 different industries. You may go through similar changes throughout your career.

A Self-Fulfilling Prophesy in Full Swing

You become too old for all of your dreams only if you feel you are too old for them. By the ages of 40, 50, and 60, some people feel life has passed them by, and they feel they are too old to go to college and earn a degree or that next degree, too old to start a business, too old to get a good-paying job, and too old to continue moving up the organization. If they truly believe that they are too old to accomplish these things, then they really are too old. That is a self-fulfilling prophesy in full swing!

Do Something

People who think that way are already half dead. They already have one foot in the grave and might just as well as put the other foot in the grave and lie down. They will lie around as couch potatoes watching television all day and just griping and moaning about all the wrong things going on in the world. Instead, they could get off their duffs and do something about it. But, they won't. They are too fixated on being losers.

The Loser's Limp

On a day in 2000, I came upon a 55-year-old man at a career center. He was hunched over, had a frown on his face, and said to me that he can't get hired because he was too old and that companies were practicing age discrimination. He had the loser's limp. Also, he said that if he ever were offered a job, they wouldn't pay him but half of what he made on his previous full-time job. What a loser! What he didn't realize was that his attitude and demeanor were the reasons why companies didn't want to hire him. He needed a paradigm shift…very badly!

No Age or Salary Discrimination

I am 63 years old today approaching 64 years old, yet I was recently hired by the Defense Acquisition University (DAU) as a full-time, tenured professor of systems acquisition management at a great salary. So, where is the age and salary discrimination?

This fall, I will be seeking an online doctor of management (DM) degree from the University of Maryland University College (UMUC), an online PhD in Educational Leadership and Higher Education (ELHE) with the University of Nebraska—Lincoln (UNL), or a DM degree with the University of Phoenix (UoP).

I have written/published 10 books over the past four years and plan to continue writing/publishing on the average of three books per year. There are many more things in which I am involved; however, lest I bore you, I'll stop here.

The Difference is in the Attitudes

So, now, can you see the difference in that 55-year-old man and what I am doing? The major difference between us is only a huge disparity in attitudes. It doesn't matter what age you are. You can do whatever you think you can, for *whatever the mind can conceive and sincerely believe can be achieved*. At the age of 63, I still have great dreams to accomplish in the remaining 37 years of my life. I say 37 years because I will live until I'm 100 years old! My dad lived until he was 89 years old, and my mom lived until she was 85. Hence, I believe I could reach 100 years old quite easily.

Consulting is a Good Career

As I had mentioned in my other answer to you, yes, there is a way for you to be more than one thing. If you think you will run out of time and time is of the essence, then do two and three things simultaneously. That's what I am doing.

You asked, "Is this what turns into consulting work?" Consulting is a great profession. I have made a lot of money consulting. When you acquire expertise in scarce fields, the demand for your services is high. Supply and demand determines how much you can charge your clients. Hence, consulting is an honorable profession and can be quite lucrative for you. Don't ever discount consulting throughout your career as a means of generating income.

Your Attitude Determines Your Altitude

In summary, if people think they are too old for accomplishing great and wonderful things in their lives, then they might just as well keel over and die. The only time we are too old for anything is when we are actually six feet under and with neither a pulse nor sustained breathing. That's when we are too old for accomplishing dreams. Remember that for the rest of your days. May the source guide you in all you do and accomplish throughout your life! Your attitude determines your altitude. So, make today the beginning of the rest of your grand life.

Finding a Successful Niche in Life

Without a doubt, earning great amounts of money has driven me to study finance. On the other hand, I am afraid of sacrificing a balanced lifestyle to work endless hours for extraordinary pay and a miserable life, yet I may be assuming incorrectly.

Further, I would enjoy finding my niche in life to be successful—a balance of health, love, success, wealth, peace, and happiness. However, I have learned to be happy and content with the people and objects that surround me.

For instance, I know I had to be a joyful Marine electrician before I moved on since the Marine Corps can be rough at times. Make no mistake about the fact that I am forever grateful for serving as a United States Marine.

Now, I understand that I should not settle for the mediocre, for I should dedicate myself toward realizing my goals—so we should be dreamers. So, what is it that has guided you through your career to find your special niche in life to be successful, regarding the career aspect of your life?

Weaknesses Become Strengths

Even though I would have liked to achieve fame, fortune, and power, these three things were not the prime motivators in my career and life. I have had good health and an overabundance of energy throughout my life, and I am very thankful to my Heavenly Father for those blessings. I was trained and disciplined by goodly parents, and I am grateful for them.

I have had many shortcomings, handicaps, inferiority complexes, and setbacks throughout my life, but I am very grateful for them because they strengthened me. These problems, trials, and tribulations have driven me to accomplish many things for good throughout life.

Service to Others is Center of Motivation

The center of my motivation has been my religion and service to others. I have spent an exorbitant amount of time in church work and serving others, particularly young people. Fortunately, I found a mate that had the same beliefs as I had, so we have had a great marriage for 38 years now and have raised three very successful, wonderful children.

Our love for God and family has been a real bond for us, which has provided us with much happiness in life. Happiness is the byproduct of service to humanity, obedience to a higher power, service to country, and working at one's passions.

Proud of Service to Country

I am very proud of my over eight years of active duty service in the USAF and four years of AFROTC. I love our country and would do everything in my power to preserve our way of life…even to laying down my life in protecting and maintaining our republic.

To me, freedom, liberty, free agency, love, peace, honor, integrity, honesty, loyalty, duty, responsibility, free enterprise, competition, capitalism, country, family, God, righteousness, friends, and faith are words that have great meaning and value.

When I watch our military personnel on TV as they unselfishly serve to preserve the peace in Afghanistan and Iraq, my eyes well with tears. My heart just swells with pride as I listen to the "National Anthem" and watch our soldiers raise the American flag at various occasions.

Patriotism Shows Pride and Honor to Country

I am filled with pride and honor whenever I hear patriotic hymns, and I feel like marching around to expend the energy so generated. "The Battle Hymn of the

Republic" brings tears to my eyes, and I want to shout Hallelujah along with the choral singers.

It saddens me that people can actually burn the American flag as a display of their freedom of speech. To me, burning the American flag has nothing to do with free speech. Speech is with the mouth; burning the American flag is done with the hands and a nasty match fueled with lighter fluid. For goodness sake, the flag represents our country and for which it stands. Those who would burn our American flag would just as soon see our country burn down...yes, the "hate America first crowd."

No Compartmentalization

My religion, family, employment, and community are interwoven together. I do not and cannot compartmentalize my life. My personal values, beliefs, philosophy, ideals, morals, and ethics cannot be compartmentalized. They all work together as a complete whole.

I cannot reverently serve in church on Sundays and then be a vastly different task-oriented person on the job during the week or when teaching our class on Tuesday evenings. Good performance on the job is important, but to have meaning, we should accomplish it as tempered with morality, honesty, responsibility, and caring.

The Scout Oath Means Much to Me

Little things, like the Boy Scout Oath (or Promise), mean so much to me. Call me square; call me weird; call me corny; call me phony; but I truly do believe in the Scout Oath, which goes as such:

> *On my honor, I will do my best*
> *To do my duty to God and my country*
> *and to obey the Scout Law;*
> *To help other people at all times;*
> *To keep myself physically strong,*
> *mentally awake, and morally straight.*

The Scout Law Uplifts My Soul

The Scout Law, also uplifts my soul, when we say, "A scout is:

- TRUSTWORTHY
   A Scout tells the truth. He keeps his promises. Honesty is part of his code of conduct. People can depend on him.

- LOYAL

  A Scout is true to his family, Scout leaders, friends, school, and nation.
- HELPFUL

  A Scout is concerned about other people. He does things willingly for others without pay or reward.
- FRIENDLY

  A Scout is a friend to all. He is a brother to other Scouts. He seeks to understand others. He respects those with ideas and customs other than his own.
- COURTEOUS

  A Scout is polite to everyone regardless of age or position. He knows good manners make it easier for people to get along together.
- KIND

  A Scout understands there is strength in being gentle. He treats others as he wants to be treated. He does not hurt or kill harmless things without reason.
- OBEDIENT

  A Scout follows the rules of his family, school, and troop. He obeys the laws of his community and country. If he thinks these rules and laws are unfair, he tries to have them changed in an orderly manner rather than disobey them.
- CHEERFUL

  A Scout looks for the bright side of things. He cheerfully does tasks that come his way. He tries to make others happy.
- THRIFTY

  A Scout works to pay his way and to help others. He saves for unforeseen needs. He protects and conserves natural resources. He carefully uses time and property.
- BRAVE

  A Scout can face danger even if he is afraid. He has the courage to stand for what he thinks is right even if others laugh at or threaten him.
- CLEAN

  A Scout keeps his body and mind fit and clean. He goes around with those who believe in living by these same ideals. He helps keep his home and community clean.
- REVERENT

  A Scout is reverent toward God. He is faithful in his religious duties. He respects the beliefs of others."

The Scout Motto Motivates Me

Also, the Scout Motto, which is "Be Prepared," motivates me. If we are always prepared, we shall not fear no matter what trials come our way or problems placed in our path.

The Scout Slogan Fosters Service

Finally, the Scout Slogan, "Do a Good Turn Daily," again, fosters the principle of service. I love everything for which the Scouting Program stands.

Pride in the Pledge to the Flag

I well with pride when we can recite the Pledge to the Flag. I love it!

> *I pledge allegiance to the Flag*
> *of the United States of America,*
> *and to the Republic for which it stands:*
> *one Nation under God, indivisible,*
> *With Liberty and Justice for all.*

Grateful for the Declaration of Independence

I am so grateful to our founding fathers when they drafted the Declaration of Independence. These words, extracted from the Declaration, make me very thankful to be an American:

> *WE hold these Truths to be self-evident, that all Men are created equal, that they are endowed by their Creator with certain unalienable Rights, that among these are Life, Liberty, and the Pursuit of Happiness.*

> *And for the support of this Declaration, with a firm Reliance on the Protection of divine Providence, we mutually pledge to each other our Lives, our Fortunes, and our sacred Honor.*

Constitution of the United States of America Stirs the Soul

I am also very grateful for the Constitution of the United States of America, which has these stirring words:

> *We the people of the United States, in order to form a more perfect union, establish justice, insure domestic tranquility, provide for the common defense, promote the*

general welfare, and secure the blessings of liberty to ourselves and our posterity, do ordain and establish this Constitution for the United States of America.

The Jaycee Creed Guides My Life

I had served in the California Jaycees and United States Jaycees for about a decade of my life in my younger days (from 25–35 years of age). With the service we gave in the Jaycees, we followed The Jaycee Creed. I believe in the Jaycee Creed. It has guided my life as has the Scout Oath and Law. The Jaycee Creed goes as follows:

> *We Believe…*
> *that faith in God gives meaning and purpose to human life,*
> *that the brotherhood of man transcends the sovereignty of nations,*
> *that economic justice can best be won by free men through free enterprise,*
> *that government should be of laws rather than of men,*
> *that earth's great treasure lies in human personality,*
> *and that Service to Humanity is the BEST WORK OF LIFE!*

I Love the USA!

I love this great country of ours from sea to shining sea. I am grateful to stand on this hallowed ground we call the United States of America. I will fight to the death to protect our great country.

I will also fight to the death to protect the rights of those who practice their freedom of speech by tearing down our country. For when the day comes that these people get snuffed out for expressing their vitriolic speech, that's the day when this country will have been taken over by the enemies of peace and freedom…enemies from both within and without the borders of this country. We must not let that happen.

We must always be vigilant to assure that our Constitution is never trampled upon and abolished by enemies who seek to eradicate us as well as to liquidate our wonderful way of life. To this end, I pledge to all my life, my fortune, and my sacred honor.

Principle-Centered Life

These ideals and principles are what have guided me throughout my career and life. These ideals and principles have helped me to find my special niche in life and to be successful in the career aspect of my life. I welcome you to do likewise in your life, i.e., to have a principle-centered life. If we always do what is right, we well never go wrong or astray. That is my promise to you.

4

Career Choice

Many people pursue certain careers because it's "what they know" or what they think they're good at. Yet all too often career choices don't lead to personal happiness on the job or to maximizing one's potential.[4]

Staff Writer
The Career News

C hoose a career that you would love doing for the rest of your life. Wouldn't it be great to get paid for having fun? If you do not have fun getting up early, going into work early, working hard all day and even through your lunch hour, and working late into the evenings, then you should change your career field.

There is nothing worse than forcing yourself to go to work every day. Find work for which you are passionate. If you do not have a fire in your belly in doing your job, then you are wasting your time and life. There is something better. Find it.

Is Your Job a "Push" or a "Pull"?

On the question for tips on "Ways to Loving your Job," I suggest you take a different twist to this. The normal approach would be to "push" the job on people. In other words, you would devise a host of ways to get (or force, coax, coerce, convince, or bamboozle) people to love their jobs. The twist I am referring to is to "pull" the people to the job. You would do this by getting people to take the requisite tests, e.g., Career Success Map Questionnaire (CSMQ), Myers-Briggs Type

---

4.   Staff Writer, "Are you on the right career path?," *The Career News*, May 22, 2006, issue, Vol. 6, Issue 22.

Indicator (BMTI), which is the same as Jung Typology Test (JTT), and/or other interest, personality, talent, and capability tests on the Internet. They are all free!

Jobs That Fit Our Passion Pull Us to Them

Next, identify your passion. Then, search for jobs that "fit" your passion. Now, these jobs "pull" you to them. Once you get one of those jobs, you will be happy doing it because you are passionate about it. *Isn't it great to get paid for having fun?* That's the trick or twist. We don't need to devise ways to get ourselves to love our jobs if we are employed in doing only those jobs for which we have a great passion. What do you think?

Be Original

You're a different kind of person. In other words, you are creative and innovative. Don't do what most people would normally do. Those are boring ways of going about things. Be different by doing creative and innovative things. Remember when I've asked the question: *Have you come up with an original thought yet today?* That's what you want to do. Be original, not a copycat or an also ran.

Get Paid for Having Fun

It's too much work to get people to love their jobs. A better way to go is to "fit" people's passion with the right job. Then, you have a motivated worker who loves his/her job. He/she becomes much more productive than otherwise. Furthermore, he/she will be happy, maintain job satisfaction, and will not go home and kick the dog, smack the kids, and yell at the spouse. All these are good results just by getting people in jobs where they *get paid for having fun.*

Making a Blurry Picture More Clear

I am graduating in the spring of 2006. My career plan is to move to New York and seek a job in the fashion industry. However, since it is an expensive place to live, family and friends have advised me to stay here for the summer and save up some money. I know you probably disagree with that idea, but I do want to be as financially stable as possible when I move. I am flexible as to when I move.

So, I am going to start sending out my resume right away. I know I want to work in the fashion industry but I am not sure exactly what job would be right for me. Marketing? Sales? Product Development? I also have not had much experience in this industry. How do you suggest going about this? Should I try for internships first?

Also, I have been offered a marketing internship through my current job at a local company called Euphora (hair products). This is not what I want to do in the long run. But do you think it would be good for the experience of working in a different and more corporate environment? In other words, I feel like I have an idea and goal of what I want to do, but the picture is blurry. How do I make it more clear?

Lay a Firm Foundation

If your real passion is a marketing, sales, or product development job in the fashion industry in New York, that is a great goal. You should find a good, relevant fashion-related job here in San Diego County upon graduating and work in it for a year or two. Learn all you can and save up as much of your earnings as possible. Then, seek a position in New York in the fashion industry while you are still working in San Diego.

Find a Job While You are Employed

Don't move to New York before you find a good job there. Finding a fashion industry job in New York while you are still employed here in San Diego is a much better approach than quitting your job here, moving to New York, and then seeking work while you are unemployed. That is the risky way to go.

Develop an Experience Base

If you do not have much experience in the fashion industry, then you must make a concerted effort to acquire such experience. An internship would be fine either during the spring semester 2006 or during the summer after you graduate. Remember, the purpose of internships is only to check you out to see if they want to hire you full time. Hence, if you do a good job as an intern, they will hire you full time. Do not take any internship not directly related to the fashion industry…even if it is with your current company.

Beef Up Your Resume

Join a couple of professional fashion organizations. Attend their meetings and get involved in the organization. Read their magazines and journals as well as other fashion periodicals. If there are certification courses/classes that you can take in fashion design, do it. Do whatever it takes to beef up your resume to make you appear to be a person involved in fashion sales, marketing, and/or product development. It's all up to you.

Caught in a Conflicting Career Battle Choice

Please help! My career and schooling were all planned out to the tee. Now there is disruption, and I am becoming worried of making the wrong decision. My plan was to finish my last two classes to receive my BSBA, moving on to pursue my Masters in Gerontology, and then to earn my Nursing Home Administrator's License. Can you tell I like to plan ahead?

I am currently actively pursuing my Residential Care Facility for the Elderly Administrator's License where my focus is not only encompassing all aspects of running and managing a community for the elderly but also on repercussions and state mandated regulations, etc.

I am becoming quite interested in the legal aspects of the business as I am being introduced to them piece by piece. This could change my entire plan and career to becoming a Licensed Program Analyst, working for the Department of Social Services conducting surveys on multiple communities. I know you cannot decide for me what job or career to change to, but any insight on this would be great. Thanks.

Career Changes

Remember this: On average, you will go through three to six career changes throughout your working lifetime. Hence, if that is the case, why worry about it? Myself? Why, I have gone through 10 career fields throughout my 40-year career thus far. Here they are:

- Aerospace engineering including R&D
- Air Force officer
- Community service
- General and executive management
- Sales, marketing, and business development
- Proposal development
- Business ownership/entrepreneurship
- Consulting
- Writing, authoring, and publishing
- Teaching and training

I have worked in the following seven industries:

- Aerospace Industry
- Defense Industry
- Electronics Industry

- Telecommunications Industry
- Software Services Industry
- Information Technology (IT) Industry
- Knowledge Industry

Alfred E. Newman

Now, I am going to date myself. You need to be like Alfred E. Newman. Do you know who he is? In *Mad Magazine*, he used to say, "What! Me worry?" Be like Alfred E. Newman. Do not worry about it. Take life as it comes. Yes, plan your career. However, be open and receptive to changing wants, needs, aspirations, motivations, passions, and/or whatever else that keeps you going.

Just Go With the Flow

As you acquire more education and gain more career experience, you will find that your desires will change. So, just go with the flow. As long as you are happy with what you are doing, you are doing just fine. Hence, when you have self-actualized in a certain job or career field and you feel it is time to get on a new learning curve, then, go for it! That's what I've done throughout my career. I tried many things…some I liked and some I didn't like so much. However, I had fun all along the journey. The journey isn't over yet. I have 37 more years to go before I reach 100.

Always Believe in Yourself

If you start from the premise that you do not make wrong career decisions, then you have no need to fear. In other words, whatever you decide, go with it at a hundred miles an hour. Then, when you are satisfied with that race, go on to the next one. You see, you will never go wrong if you sincerely believe that whatever you do is the right thing for you at that time-period.

Even if you may fail at whatever choice you made, you will learn a lot from it, which will help you in the future. Heaven knows, I have made many choices of which outcomes may be considered by others as unsuccessful or failures. However, failures provide much knowledge and wisdom to write and teach about in my present knowledge-based profession.

Baseball Greats Bat .333 or Higher

Look at it this way, top baseball greats hit only one out of three times at bat. Achieving a batting average of 33.3 percent would be a dismal failure in other professions. However, we consider baseball players who bat .333 or higher as great hitters and/or sluggers.

Can you imagine a brain surgeon with a 33.3 percent success rate? No patient would ever allow such a brain surgeon to operate on her/him. Can you imagine an aircraft, bridge, or high-rise building designer with only 33.3 percent of his stress calculations done correctly? Who would want to fly in such an airplane, cross such a bridge, or live in such a building? I wouldn't. Would you?

Be Like a Baseball Player

Therefore, be like a baseball player. Say, you make only two out of three correct career choices. It doesn't matter. Turn a poor choice into a good choice by learning a lot from it and about it. *Bad choices and failure help you to gain wisdom.* If you were successful at everything you did, you wouldn't appreciate it as much as you wouldn't have a contrast of where you came from and where you are going. My career has been a roller coaster ride, and it has been a lot of fun. So, enjoy your ride over the next 40 or so years. When you are all done, tell me about it.

Look for a Certain Position or Enter a Management Trainee Program

If I already have a variety of previous work experience (although not really managerial), should I look for a certain position coming out of college, or should I go into a management trainee program? These trainee programs usually pay less than what I am making and seem to target those that are coming out of college with minor or no work experience. What is your take on this?

You Will Make Whatever You Value Yourself

Look for a good, solid position coming out of college. Only if you cannot be successful at that, then your fallback position would be to seek a management trainee program. Management trainee programs will pay you anywhere from $30K-$35K/year; whereas, a good, solid position coming out of college should get you $35K-$40K/year. The average BSBA graduate should be able to get about $40K/year today. If you are really good and have a lot to offer, you could make $40K-$45K/year starting out. It's up to you. Whatever you value yourself at is what you will be able to command.

Your Fit

Your CSMQ shows you are strong on "Getting Ahead" and "Getting Balanced." Your JTT/MBTI is an ENFJ extrovert, and you are a very strong extrovert. You would make a very good executive, salesman, teacher, or therapist. Both your resume objective and personal brand statement (PBS) indicate that you want to be a leader. Your resume shows you have been a salesman at Garcia Farms and a sales consultant at Sears. Everything fits. Your sales experience fits in with your being an extrovert and your desire to be a great leader fits with your "Getting Ahead" orientation.

Management Trainee Program

Basically, the management trainee program is designed to get a lot of good work out of people at a cheaper price. You can get as much management training by getting a good management job in a good company. Some students already have or have had management positions. You can too. Work towards that end. Take a management trainee position only if you cannot find a good, suitable management position or a position that would quickly lead to a management position.

One Step Backwards; Two Steps Forward

I have been continuing to look for positions that fit what I want to do, which seems to have become more and more broad. I have maintained contact with a classmate and became interested in his company (Wells Fargo), which I just interviewed with yesterday. I was offered the position, but I told them that I would need time for consideration as I have also interviewed with another company. I really like what Wells Fargo has to offer me, but I also feel as though it is not directly related to the field I wish to pursue, which is marketing. Because of this, I am taking this weekend to look over everything. I'll let you know how it goes!

Sometimes We Need to Punt

What is this other company (other than Wells Fargo) with which you had interviewed? Is it a good company? Remember, what I had said once before? *Sometimes, we need to take a step backwards to take two steps forward.* Hence, if the other company doesn't work out, you may need to take the Wells Fargo offer, work there for a year or two, and then move into a job you want in the field of your dreams.

> *Sometimes, we need to take a step backwards to take two steps forward.*

Better to Search for a Job While Employed

While employed at Wells Fargo, you will have all the time you need to search for the job of your dreams. Remember, *it's better to look for a job while you are employed than when you are unemployed.* Furthermore, you don't want too much time to go by since you graduated in May before you start working for a good company. Wells Fargo is a good company to acquire some basic training and experience under your belt. You can also get into more marketing-oriented positions in Wells Fargo.

> *It's better to look for a job while you are employed than when you are unemployed.*

Azhoon Abdulghani—a Successful Man

For example, say you start at Wells Fargo working as a teller. Then, if you are sharp (as you are), you can be promoted to a loan specialist and learn about loaning and acquiring loan accounts. You can also get into marketing in the Wells Fargo Bank as did Azhoon Abdulghani (one of my outstanding spring 2004 students), who spoke to our class in the fall 2004 semester. You can sell or market bank products and/or services. Basically, Azhoon is involved in marketing as an assistant vice president and branch manager of Wells Fargo Bank! You can do likewise. Azhoon (who is about 26 years old) graduated with you in May 2005.

Heather Uda Meier

My daughter, Heather, obtained a teller job at Washington Mutual Bank fresh out of high school. She worked hard, got several promotions, ended up as a senior personal financial representative in that bank within three years, and she did very well in four years at the bank. From there, she went on to manage a 97-unit apartment complex making over $50K/year (without a college degree).

More Than One Way to Skin a Cat

Two-and-a-half years later, she is now back with Washington Mutual selling loans, where she has the potential of making over $100K/year! I told her that she needs to go to college and earn a business degree to validate (after the fact) her position and potential income. She agrees. Remember, *there is more than one way to skin a cat.*

5

Dream Job and Passion

Find something you love to do, and you'll never have to work a day in your life.

Harvey Mackay, Newspaper Columnist,
Author, and Business Motivational Speaker

Discover your true passion or passions. Then, find the job and career field that would satisfy your passion. If you find your dream job, you will do extremely well in it because you will be happy and productive. You will basically be paid for having fun. What a way to live! Getting paid for having fun is the best way to go. So, always pursue your passion.

How Can I Go About Discovering My True Passion in Life?

I am currently a senior at Cal State San Marcos, and I will graduate in December 2005. I have thoroughly enjoyed working hard to obtain my BSBA degree at Cal State San Marcos. The only problem that I have is that I have not found one area of study more appealing than another. I am at a crossroads trying to figure out what career path to choose.

I have attended class after class listening to lectures about pursuing your passion. The only problem is that I haven't discovered my passion yet. My plan, thus far, is to apply for jobs that I believe I will like and, hopefully, discover my passion through these types of experiences. Are there any suggestions you can give me to help me narrow down career choices I may make in the future in order to help guide me to the path of discovering my true passion in life?

Don't Be Short Sighted

You should always go for your passion. People who take a job they hate but that pays a lot of money are short sighted. Yes, in the beginning, you may make more money then your peers, but, eventually, you will get bored, frustrated, and tired

41

of your job. Then, your attitude goes down, your performance declines, and you become ripe for the next reduction in force (RIF). Plus that, you may become pigeonholed and would find it extremely difficult to transfer into a different career field.

Do What You are Passionate About

On the other hand, if you do what you are passionate about, you will be happier with your work and, consequently, you will do superior work. Starting out, you may not make as much money as your peers. However, as you improve and get better and better, you may end up making much more money than otherwise, particularly if you become "world class" in what you do.

Self-Actualize Continuously

If you pursue work that you are passionate about, life will be great for you. You will epitomize the statement: *"Isn't it great getting paid for having fun?"* That's what you want to do in your career. Find out what you are passionate about and then seek the kind of work that satisfies your passion. You will continually self-actualize throughout your career and life.

> *Isn't it great getting paid for having fun?*

Cost-Benefit Analysis

Now, in determining whether you should take a lower amount (if that is the offeror's best and final salary offer) for a job you are passionate above, you should conduct a cost-benefit analysis. Determine all of the pros and cons of taking the job. Then, evaluate whether the opportunity cost will be offset by the benefits you will receive.

Opportunity Cost

Opportunity cost is the value of the opportunity that you lose or sacrifice when you choose to take the lower salary with a job you love as contrasted to taking a job you hate but at a higher salary. By working in the job you love, if the fun and enjoyment you receive far supersedes the loss of salary, then take the lower salary and do not look back.

Plow forward and do well in your great new job. As you do that, you will accomplish fantastic and wonderful things. You will notice that your promo-

> *Go with your passion.*

tions and salary increases eventually will far exceed what you would receive in the initially higher-paying but lousy job. The moral of the story is to *go with your passion.*

Get Paid for Having Fun

You will always do better on what you are passionate about than on other things that you are not as passionate about. Yes, you can do something well that you are not passionate about and make good money at it. However, if you work at what you are passionate about, though you may start out making less money at first, you can and will do better with passing time and ultimately will make good money at it. *Isn't it great to be paid for having fun?* That is what professional sports folks do. They play at their jobs and make very good money at it. They receive lots of money just for having fun!

Be "World Class" at Whatever You Do

No matter what occupation it is, if you can be the best in the world at it, the world will make a beaten path to your door even though you live deep in the woods. So, if you make mouse traps, be the best mousetrap maker in the world. If you are going to be a garbage man, be the best garbage man in the world. If you are going to be a cook, be the best cook in the world. In other words, be *"world class at whatever you decide to do."* If you do that, the money will automatically flow towards you.

> *Be world class at whatever you decide to do.*

Making Good Money

Being the best in the world at whatever you do is easier and more fun if you have a deep passion for it. The best surfers in the world make good money. The best musicians in the world make good money. The best bodybuilders in the world make good money. The best golfers in the world make good money. The best artists in the world make good money. The best chess players in the world make good money. We can go on and on and cover every occupation no matter how mundane or esoteric it may be.

Outdo Your Peers

So, identify your passion. Start working at it in a job. You may start out making a low salary or wage that does not pay the bills. However, with the passage of time, you will get better and better at it. When you do, your salary or wage will increase accordingly. However, you need to continue studying about it and practicing at it. You need to work more at it than all of your peers or competitors. You need to spend more time at it. You need to get expert advice about it. You need to visualize yourself growing and becoming the best at it. Through blood, sweat, tears, and perseverance, you will ultimately achieve the success you seek.

Pay Your Dues

Don't put the cart before the horse. You must pay your dues. You must start with the basics. You must build a firm foundation. You must start with the building blocks. You must invest the requisite time. You must sacrifice by forgoing doing other fun things. Progress will be slow at first. However, as you come down the learning curve, you will get better and better at it. You will be able to do more in less time and at better quality. You become more efficient, more proficient, more productive, and more effective.

> *Don't put the cart before the horse.*

If You Do What You Love, You Will Love What You Do

I say, do what you love to do. Yes, you may not make much money at it starting out. However, if you strive diligently at being world class at it, you will eventually make good money. *If you do what you love, you will love what you do.* You will also be happy or happier working on your passion than you would ever be even if you were doing well working at what you hate. Too many people go to work every day hating what they do. They feel trapped because they either cannot do anything else or won't give up the high income they are making and settle for much less income but loving what they do.

> *If you do what you love, you will love what you do.*

Bite the Bullet

If they changed their occupation and did something that they loved, they would need to take one half, one third, or even, maybe, one fourth of what they are currently making. That, in and of itself, discourages most people from making a job change. Thus, they continually go about doing the same old boring job every day and hating it all the while because they will not *"bite the bullet"* and do what they would love to do at half the income.

Top Gun—Best of the Best

Do you remember the movie titled "Top Gun"? Those Navy pilots were the "best of the best." That is what we need to do, i.e., to be the best of the best at anything and everything we do. I once worked with several retired former Top Gun pilots. Everything they did, they worked at being the "best of the best." It is an attitude ingrained in their psyche. With an attitude like that, they will be successful at whatever they do. You can do likewise.

> *Be the best of the best.*

Follow Your Passion

Hence, if you follow your passion and do what you love to do, you will do well at it. You will also be happy at what you do, and you will be successful. The money will eventually flow your way.

Find Jobs That Fit Your Passion

You first need to know what is your passion. Then, you need to identify the jobs that are of your dreams, the industry they are in, and the companies these jobs are in. Go on the *Internet* to the major job searching sites and find those jobs that satisfy your passion. Then, go after those jobs.

Network for Your Dream Job

Simultaneously, *network* with all of the people who have, know about, and desire those dream jobs. Use your network to identify unpublished job vacancies. Work your network to obtain interviews for these jobs. Capture one of those dream jobs.

Prepare Yourself

Also, simultaneously, do everything you can to *prepare yourself*, your resume, and your reputation such that everyone will know that you are the best person to fill that dream job. If you have all of the tickets and all of the blocks on the application form checked, you maximize your probability of being hired for that dream job.

> *"…if you build the best thingamajig in the world, though your home may be located deep in the woods, the world will make a beaten path to your door."*

The World Will Seek You Out

If you are "*world class*" or the best in the world at whatever is your dream job, the world will seek you out to fill that dream job. You won't need to look for and find the job of your dreams. Also, if you build the best *thingamajig* in the world, though your home may be located deep in the woods, the world will make a beaten path to your door.

Getting Ahead

Looking at your CSMQ orientation, you have a strong 11 at "Getting Ahead." You will quest for the top of the organizational hierarchy and status system. You will focus on upward mobility, status, and power. That's you, and it fits!

You Excel in Service Occupations

Now, looking at your JTT/MBTI code, you are an ESFJ extrovert. You like harmony. You tend to have strong "shoulds" and "should-nots." You may be dependent, first on your parents and later on your spouse. You wear your heart on your sleeve and excel in service occupations involving personal contact.

Your Strengths

Some of your strengths include being a cooperative person, obedient, well organized, and good with facts. You take the personal approach at work and are hard working and productive. You are conscientious and loyal, and you adapt well to routine.

Your Weaknesses

Some of your weaknesses include being sensitive to criticism, stressed by tense work situations, and can become discouraged without praise. If working alone, you may become restless and may not look for new ways to do things. At times, you can be opinionated and rigid.

Recommendation

With these facts, I think you should work in a service occupation. I guess that's why you are concentrating in the Service Sector on your BSBA degree, right? So, select a service occupation that allows you to be scheduled, organized, systematic, methodical, decisive, and unstressed. Additionally, look for a job that will require you to prepare short- and long-term plans.

Seeking Jobs that are Exciting and High Risk

I am not interested in climbing corporate ladders and performing common jobs. I need something constantly exciting to maintain my interest. I have always participated in extreme sports and activities in pursuit of adrenalin and instant gratification. Financial security is important to me but less so than is avoiding monotony. I think I may be interested in marketing or, further, entrepreneurship because I like the risk involved. Are you aware of any steady careers or jobs that would suit my needs?

Jobs to Pursue

You could consider looking into the following jobs:

- Driver in auto races
- Movie stunt man
- Navy Seal
- Pilot with the Blue Angels precision demonstration team
- Trader on Wall Street
- Speedboat racer
- Astronaut
- Infantry officer in Iraq
- Espionage agent with the Central Intelligence Agency (CIA)
- Captain of the Los Angeles Special Weapons and Tactics (SWAT) Team

Getting Balanced

Though you express interest in non-boring, exciting, and high-risk jobs, it is interesting to note that on your Career Success Map Questionnaire (CSMQ), your orientation is very strong (10) on "getting balanced." "Getting balanced" means you seek meaningful balance among work, important relationships, and personal development; furthermore, you focus on flexibility and efficiency.

Getting High

Next, you had a low 4 on "getting high," which is a desire for excitement, "cutting edge" opportunities, and adventure; focus on challenging projects and passionate causes. This is where you should be from what you say you truly desire. However, you are a "getting balanced" guy.

Never in Business!

Furthermore, on the Myers-Briggs Type Indicator (MBTI) or Jung Typology Test (JTT), you are an INFP, which states you are idealistic, self-sacrificing, and somewhat cool or reserved. You are very family and home oriented (which matches your "getting balanced" in the CSMQ), but you don't relax well. You should work well in psychology, architecture, and religion, but never in business!

A Disconnect

Therefore, there appears to be somewhat of a disconnect between what you say you want to do and what your CSMQ and MBTI/JTT scores say you really are.

Should I Go for the Money or My Passion?

As others have mentioned, this class has been a real "eye opener" for me. It has made me think of many things in my future career. Currently, I like where I work, the pay, benefits, and working hours. However, I do not see myself in this position for the rest of my life. I want to move up the ladder or go for my passion job. See, this is where my question lies.

I do not work in the field that I want to work in, which is in HR, nor do I have any experience in this field. Having said this, I've done research on how much I can potentially be making in this field, and it is nothing comparable to what I am currently making. Thus, I would be taking a major cut in pay. I know you've mentioned in class that we should do something we like and have a passion for, but is it worth taking what it seems to me as a huge pay cut to go after your passion job?

I consider myself a risk taker, but when it comes to pay, benefits, and the working environment, I ask myself this question: Is it worth me leaving this job for something that will pay me less and taking the risk of entering a new environment?

Money is a Motivator

No matter how much you say you want an HR passion job, you still indicate that money is an even greater motivator to you. You have made the following statements:

- You say, "I like where I work, the pay, benefits, and working hours."
- You've "…done research on how much I can potentially be making in this field, and it is nothing comparable to what I am currently making."
- You state, "I would be taking a major cut in pay."

- You also state, "…but is it worth taking what it seems to me as a huge pay cut to go after your passion job?"
- You further state, "…but when it comes to pay, benefits, and the working environment, I ask myself this question: Is it worth me leaving this job for something that will pay me less and taking the risk of entering a new environment?"

Money is Important to You

Can you see that you have stated five concerns about making less money? Therefore, money is very important to you. If you have no experience in HR, how do you really know that it is your passion job? After you get into HR, you may find that it is not all cracked up to be what you had thought it would be. Then, you will be unhappy in a lower paying job, hating every minute of it, and dreaming of the higher paying job you had left. You need to determine if HR really is your passion.

Human Resources

Remember, HR is a staff position, not a line position. They are indirect, not direct. They, basically, spend money. They don't make money for the company. However, they do periodically recruit top-notch employees who do bring money into the company, so there is a plus from that standpoint.

Your Doubts are Revealing

From all of your statements above about your doubts about HR, I really don't see it as your true passion. The only way you will make good money in HR is if you become a director or vice president of HR. Those people are usually scarce. The rest are grunts doing the work at much lower salaries. Money cannot be a motivator when you work in HR. There must be other altruistic things in HR that are attractive you.

Go Into Fields That Pay Good Money

If money is truly a motivator to you, then you should get into these fields (which make money):

- Engineering
- Marketing and sales
- General management
- Finance

- Computer design
- Medicine
- Law

Stay out of HR

HR is not the occupation where you will make big bucks. So, if money is your driver, stay out of HR.

The Money Will Take Care of Itself

Actually, if you become "world class" in any career field that you get into, you will make a lot of money. Hence, whatever you decide to do, be the "best of the best" at it. Then, the money will take care of itself.

Your Personality

I checked your Career Success Map Questionnaire (CSMQ) results, and you are strong in "getting balanced." Hence, you desire a meaningful balance among work, important relationships, and personal development. You also focus on flexibility and efficiency. Now, looking at your Myers-Briggs Type Indicator (MBTI) or Jung Typology Test (JTT) result, you are an ENFJ, which is extroverted feeling with intuiting. These people are easy speakers. They tend to idealize their friends. They make good parents but have a tendency to allow themselves to be used. They make good therapists, teachers, executives, and sales people.

Food for Thought

Thus, I don't see in your CSMQ and MBTI/JTT results a passion for becoming an HR specialist. However, I do see you being a therapist, teacher, executive, and/or sales person. Are you sure HR is your passion? You have never worked in that field. We usually determine our passion after working in a particular career field for a while and find that we really love it. Please accept my comments as just *food for thought*. Hence, think about these things and then decide which way to go.

Deciding Between the Business World or Passionate Church Service

I have really enjoyed being in the College of Business, have been a successful salesman applying many learned principles to my sales business, and have, previous to this summer, been very excited about getting out and pursuing a career in the business world.

However, lately, I have been asking myself the question, "For what?" Just before this last summer, I took an internship position with my church working with youth and leading the worship band. I have found this 'job' to be incredibly rewarding, and a job that, even though I was putting in around sixty hours a week, didn't seem like work. I have a passion for this, and my passion for playing music is also satisfied in this position.

Now I am having a hard time with my sales job, just feeling like it is pretty meaningless in the big scheme of things. I am still working at the church, and I still love it, but obviously the pay isn't anything that great. Hence, I am having conflicting feelings about whether I should stay working here, or if I need to be going out and trying to get an internship where I would be able to obtain some valuable business experience. Do you have any suggestions or insights?

Pursue Your Passion

I always tell people to pursue their passion. This is because I have been in the business world for the past 40 years and have finally settled on the areas of my passion, i.e., teaching, writing/publishing, researching, career coaching, consulting, and entrepreneurship...all of these are in the knowledge industry. So, my suggestion to you is to pursue your passion.

Become World Class at Your Passion

If you pursue your passion and become world class at it, the necessary and sufficient income will follow. If your passion is building mousetraps, and you build the finest mousetraps in the world, although you may live deep in the woods, *the world will make a beaten path to your door.* The Reverend Billy Graham followed his passion for over a half century and has made a good livelihood at it. His son, Franklin, is following in his footsteps.

Be the Best of the Best

Besides the Grahams, John Paul II followed his passion. Mother Teresa followed her passion. Mahatma Gandhi followed his passion. Reverend Jerry Falwell follows his passion. Dr. Pat Robertson follows his passion. President Gordon B. Hinckley follows his passion. Many great church leaders both past and present have followed their passion and have been quite successful at it. All you need to do is to *"be the best of the best"* in whatever you do, and you will be both successful at it and make a good livelihood at it.

Similar Passions

I too have a passion for church work and church service. For the past 40 years, I have been actively and heavily engaged in my church serving in teaching, leadership, and administrative positions working primarily with youth and young single adults (YSAs).

For the past 4 years, I served as bishop in my church with stewardship over a congregation (called a ward) of approximately 350 YSA members and have spent anywhere from 25–40 hours per week on church work. Also, I had served as a bishop once before of a traditional family ward for over 6 years. Hence, just as a bishop alone, I have given a total of 10 years and 2 months of service.

Service Provided at No Remuneration

One difference about my church service, however, is I don't get paid for it. It is purely a labor of love. In fact, I donate to the church anywhere from 10–15 percent of my gross income and have done so for the past 35 years or so. Obviously, it must be a passion for me to spend the time, energy, and money that I have in working with the youth and young adults of the church.

Career of Passion

Hence, if you have found it to be incredibly rewarding to serve in your church working with youth and leading the worship band, then that's the kind of work you should do as your *"career of passion."* Even though the pay, as you say, isn't anything that great, you are at least getting paid something and receiving an income for your 60-hour weeks of *"getting paid for having fun."*

Try Serving for No Pay

Would you still do this church service if you got paid nothing and even had to pay the church 10–15 percent of your income instead? That'll really reveal whether it is a true passion for you or not. I pay for having fun, not get paid for having fun. A consolation I have is that for my church work and service, *"the pay is terrible, but the retirement benefits are out of this world,"* if you get my drift. ☺

Simultaneously Work and Serve

What you can do is what I did. You can work in your church as well as have a day job. In fact, I have held several day jobs in addition to my church service/work. I taught at CSUSM as an adjunct faculty lecturer. I ran my consulting and career coaching business, Bob Uda and Associates. Further, I had a writing and publishing business called Buda Books Publishing.

In October 2005, I was hired as professor of systems acquisition management with the Defense Acquisition University (DAU). I did all of that to provide a roof over our heads and food on the table while simultaneously serving in my church responsibilities. You can do likewise.

Recommendation

Therefore, here is what I recommend to you. Pursue your passion with your church service work as well as pursue your sales business. Hopefully, some day, you will become financially independent; then you can focus most of your time on passionate church service. Does that make sense to you? Remember, there is always *"more than one way to skin a cat."* It can be done if you really want it bad enough. Go make it happen!

Tactical vs. Strategic Approach

Throughout the Career Development class, we have heard numerous guest speakers. One in particular, Kim Martin, stands out in my mind because she inspired me to reconsider my plans for after college. Originally, I was going to try to create a position for myself within my current company.

My question is this: Should I consider taking a job with a company such as Enterprise, where I can move up quickly and gain management experience, or should I stay with my current company because I am interested in the industry? My current company has more long-term potential, but Enterprise offers quick initial growth. Also, would it be bad to work at Enterprise for the experience, then try to go back to my current company?

Determine and Pursue Your Passion

The first thing you need to do is to determine your passion. For what career field or job do you possess great passion? Then, pursue your passion. If you pursue your passion, you will be happy with working throughout your career. Therefore, pursue your passion!

Tactical or Strategic Approach

Next, you can choose taking an either tactical or strategic approach to your career. The tactical approach looks at the short term. You look for a lot of money first whether the job interests you or not or whether it is fun or not. Remember the maxim: *"Isn't it great to get paid for having fun?"* Another way of saying it is this: *"It's great to get paid for having fun!"* To do that, you must work in the area of your passion.

Strategic Approach

The strategic approach takes the long-range view of things. You aren't concerned so much about making a lot of money quickly as you are more interested in pursuing your passion and having fun at it. Job happiness is more important to you than making a lot of money. In the long haul, if you will work to become "world class" and the "best of the best," the money will automatically flow to you. If you are the best in the world at whatever you do, people will pay you well for it.

Enterprise Rent-A-Car

Now, let's get back to your questions. If gaining good management experience is your passion, work for Enterprise. If working in the auto rental business is your passion, work for Enterprise. If quick initial growth and moving up quickly is your passion, work for Enterprise.

Current Company

If your interest in your current company's industry is your passion, stay with your current company. If your passion is long-term potential, which your company offers, stay with your current company.

Don't Go Back to a Company You Left

If you leave a company to go to another, it is usually not a good idea to go back to the company you left. When you leave, it shows a bit of disloyalty, and some people don't like that. Thus, when you return, you are at a decided disadvantage with these people. There are many good companies out there. Go to work for a better company.

Your Current Company

If your current company is so good (as you imply by desiring to return to it after leaving for a while), why don't they provide you with the advancement and management experience that Enterprise would provide you? If your current company does not promote quickly, that indicates you will be in grunt positions for a long time before they move you into management.

You Must Decide

I cannot make the decision for you. You must make the decision yourself as to staying with your current company or going with Enterprise. It seems that you are not definitely sure of your true passion. You need to determine that, and then find the job, company, and industry in which you would fit best. You may need to find a job and company in a different area than both Enterprise and your current company.

Think Strategic, Not Tactical

In conclusion, find your true passion and pursue it. Think long term, not short term. Find a job that you will have fun while being paid for the work. That is my counsel to you. Go do it!

6

Job Searching

Looking for work can be a full-time job in itself. The longer you look, the harder it is to stay positive and focused. To make it easier, organize your search and make creative use of your time.[5]

Abridged: eHow.com

If you are unemployed, searching for a good job should be your number one priority. Of course, if you are independently wealthy, you won't need to heed this advice. However, if you are like most people, you need to work, earn money, and provide for your next meal for yourself and your family. *Searching for a new job should be a full-time job.* So, take things seriously and methodically plan and pursue that next great job of yours.

> *Searching for a new job should be a full-time job.*

Is it a Good Idea to Take a Two-month Vacation after Graduation before Starting a Job Search?

My question regards those of us who would like to travel a bit before diving right into the business world. I will be graduating in December and then traveling for two months to Australia and Southeast Asia.

When would it be appropriate for me to send out my resume? What is the proper etiquette in relaying this intention to potential employers without giving them the

---

5. Abridged: eHow.com, "Organize for a more effective job search," May 22, 2006, issue of *The Career News*, Vol. 6, Issue 22.

wrong idea about me (I am not a slacker)? Thank you very much for any ideas you could give me.

Find That Job First!

If you were working in the business world for five or more years and then experienced a layoff, taking a two-month vacation before starting a job search is one of the worst things any job seeker could do. The job searcher should first find a good job, work for a while, and then take a vacation. *It is better to search for work when employed than when unemployed.* If you are a seasoned worker, do not take a vacation upon layoff. Find that job first!

It May Take Up to a Year or More to Find a New Job

Alternatively, however, when someone in the job market for a while experiences a layoff, she may have received a nice severance check. Hence, she may decide to take a month's vacation before starting a job search. She thinks that she will find a job within two months after returning from vacation. In many cases, to her surprise, it may take her up to a year or more to find a new job!

> *It is better to search for work when employed than when unemployed.*

Different Situation for New Graduates

However, since you will be a newly graduating senior seeking real-world work for the first time, we have a different situation. When a previous student asked a guest speaker from Enterprise Rent-A-Car this same question, the guest speaker said that it would not be a big deal to take that vacation. Of course, the guest speaker was in a recruiting mode; hence, her answer may be somewhat biased.

Probably Acceptable to Take a Vacation

For brand new college graduates, what the Enterprise Rent-A-Car recruiter said would probably be acceptable. However, if I were a new college graduate, I would not take a vacation. Of course, that is just me talking…a striving, quasi-workaholic who never normally takes any vacations. My vacations have been the durations of time when I was unemployed and spending 10–18 hours a day looking for a new job!

Different Story for More Seasoned Employees

The older you become and the higher on the corporate rung you reside, the more difficult it is and the longer it takes to get a good job. That is because you are:

- Making more money
- Seeking higher-level jobs
- Competing in a much stiffer competitive environment than the one for entry-level jobs

Go for It!

Because of what the guest speaker said, the decision as to what you should do is yours to make. Only you know what is good for you. You should always strive to work for a company with the great attitude that Enterprise Rent-A-Car has regarding taking a vacation between graduating and starting a new job. I say go for it!

Start Sending Out Your Resumes Now

Assuming that you do take the two-month vacation, say in January and February, the time for you to start sending out your resumes is right now. It will take you about three months to land a good position. Chances are you will not receive an offer to start working in December. Because of the holidays, not many companies hire in late November and throughout December. They nearly always push the hire-on dates to January or February. Thus, you want to receive an offer as soon as possible.

Inform the Employer During the Offer-Negotiation Process

The best time to inform the employer about your intended two-month vacation prior to starting work is during the offer-negotiation process. If most companies were anything like Enterprise Rent-A-Car, they would be amenable to your taking the two months off before starting to work. They would just move your start date to some time in March. Hey, why don't you go to work for Enterprise Rent-A-Car!

Critical Jobs Would Present a Problem

Usually, the only time you would have a problem is if you were filling a critical job that required you to be there yesterday. Then, the company may be a little reluctant to allow you to take the time off before starting the new job.

However, as a newly minted BSBA degree holder, the hiring company probably will not offer you a critical job with the need for an immediate start date. Therefore, have fun in Australia (down under) and Southeast Asia!

Getting a Job in the Makeup Industry with No Resume Experience

I have a question about trying to switch the kind of career I am currently in so that I can have at least a year of experience by the time I graduate with my business degree. I was hired on as a teller at San Diego County Credit Union at the age of 19 when I wasn't really sure what I wanted to do with my life. I have stuck with that job for the last seven years because I was continually promoted and made pretty good money.

I am currently a loan and new account rep, and now, I really know that I want to be a makeup artist and want to run my own business one day. I feel like my business degree and knowledge with school will help with this, but I really don't have the makeup experience except for what I have done on the side on my own. I do have sales experience in my current job, which is helpful with the makeup industry since a large part of their job is sales.

When I have done makeup for friends, family, and co-workers, they are always impressed and love the job I do. I just don't have the extensive training usually required for this kind of position. I feel if I was hired somewhere, I would take off and do very well once properly trained. How would I go about getting a job or even an interview for that matter in the makeup industry with no resume experience yet?— Angela Smith

Developing the Requisite Experience

This is a tough problem because the career field you desire to work in is highly specialized, doesn't have many open opportunities, and is difficult to gain the requisite experience. Thus, what you need to do is the following:

- **Acquire Experience.** Acquire as much of the directly applicable makeup experience that you can by doing the following:
  - *Self-Employment.* Start a sole proprietorship now and create a great makeup artist company name—start developing your own experience
  - *Freelance Work.* Continue to do makeup for friends, family, and co-workers and keep a record of the hours worked and the people you worked on. This work (even if unpaid or meagerly paid) will become

part of your business. You'll be acquiring real world experience through an official organization.

o *Makeup Events.* Hold your own makeup events. This will be part of your business too.

- **Networking.** Network extensively in the makeup industry by doing the following:
  o *Professional Events.* Attend makeup trade shows, conferences, seminars, workshops, and expositions.
  o *Professional Organizations.* Join makeup organizations, attend their meetings, and serve in offices in those organizations. Place the names of those organizations on your resume.

- **Publications.** Obtain makeup books, magazines, journals, and other publications and periodicals and read all of them to get super-smart on the makeup industry and in being a makeup artist.

- **Certification.** Search for makeup schools on the Internet and take short courses, get certified, and gain hands-on experience in their labs.

- **Internship.** Seek a makeup internship.

- **Fringe Jobs.** Secure part-time jobs working on the fringes of the makeup industry to acquire relevant experience and develop transferable skills. Jobs such as the following "may" (some of these may not be good because they are just wild guesses on my part and also my not being a makeup artist expert) help you build up the kind of experience that would be useful in enhancing your capabilities and track record:
  o Actor
  o Artist/Painter
  o Barber
  o Color coordinator
  o Cosmetics salesperson
  o Cosmetologist
  o Costume designer
  o Dietician
  o Designer
  o Events coordinator/wedding planner
  o Exercise coach
  o Graphic artist
  o Hairdresser/hairstylist
  o Interior decorator
  o Manicurist

- o   Masseuse
- o   Model
- o   Model maker
- o   Personal coach
- o   Personal trainer
- o   Photographer
- o   Physical therapist
- o   Sculpture artist
- o   Seamstress

Extensive Networking Needed

My guess is that the makeup industry is a close-knit industry. You need connections to get a good job within that industry. Therefore, you will need to get to know prime movers in the industry and get them to know you. Extensive networking is the way to do that.

Summary of Things to Do

In summary, you not only need to gain the:

(1) *Knowledge* by:
    a.   Reading the applicable magazines and journals
    b.   Taking seminars, workshops, and specialized schools
    c.   Getting licensed and/or certified and
(2) *Experience* through:
    a.   Internships or apprenticeships,
    b.   Performing small freelance jobs,
    c.   Starting your own firm, and
    d.   Getting your first big break, but you also need the
(3) *Exposure* by:
    a.   Participating in makeup artist professional organizations,
    b.   Attending large public gatherings of these makeup specialists, and
    c.   Networking with those who can give you that first big break.

Writing and Publishing to Become an Instant Expert

You might also write papers on the subject to present at makeup conferences and to get them published in makeup artist magazines and journals. Why don't you write a book on the subject and become an instant expert? You also acquire instant credibility.

Acquire the Specialized Knowledge and Experience Needed

You have excellent sales and business knowledge and experience. Generally, the three years you had worked in a bakery and café, seven years in banking, and a solid college education in business administration all will help you to get a good job. However, you now need to acquire the specialized knowledge and experience in the makeup industry for you to secure a good job in that industry. So, work towards that end by considering the things I have mentioned in the above list.

How Employers Look at Length of Time in Previous Jobs

I had a summer internship with Geico Insurance just this past season. The position started at a competitive pay, and originally, I was very excited that I landed the job before I completed my degree. Recently, I have decided it is not the job for me. I learned that I cannot stand staring at a computer for eight hours a day, and that a cubicle is an unhealthy place for me.

I understand that I must take the time to find the right job for me, but I am concerned that if I spend the next five years looking for the right job, my resume will look like I cannot stay employed at any one location for a long period of time. How much do employers take into consideration the length of time you have been employed at previous jobs?

Time You Should Spend in a Job

You should always attempt to stay in a job for at least a year but never less than a year. You come down the learning curve during your first year on the job. You are most productive during the second year. You should never stay in the same job for more than three years. So, after two years, start looking for your next growth assignment.

> *Always attempt to stay in a job for at least a year but never less than a year.*

Try to Stay Within the Same Company

This does not imply that you need to go immediately to another company. You should find another growth job within the same company. You should continue in the same company as long as they either promote or transfer you into a better job within the company every two to three years. If you are unable to grow in the same company, then you should start looking for a better job in another company.

When Employers Do Not Look Negatively Upon Yearly Job Changes

If you had a new job every year, employers do not look negatively upon it if:

- Each succeeding job was a promotion and demonstrated career growth
- You acquired more responsibility, authority, and salary with each succeeding job
- Each subsequent job title indicates growth

When Employers Look Negatively Upon Yearly Job Changes

What you need to watch for is to show instability through:

- Making less salary than before
- Having less authority/responsibility in subsequent jobs
- Receiving worse job titles with each job change

This kind of work record does not indicate growth and/or progress. It shows one or more of the following negative traits:

- You cannot hold on to a job for very long
- You are unstable and cannot stay in the same job for any extended length of time
- You are difficult to get along with
- You are quickly bored and are off to the next thing (flighty)

Achieve Negotiating Advantage

This is how it is in the corporate world. Plan your career and implement your plan so that you will be able to achieve the negotiating advantage (i.e., leverage) required to get your next better job. If you do not work to do this, you will have a haphazard career record.

Getting Through the Red Tape with Online Application Forms

I am wondering what I should do. I am trying to apply for a job as a makeup artist, but the only way to apply is online. I filled out the online application; however, I do not feel it gives me a way to really differentiate myself since there is no way of attaching a resume or elaborating on my talents and experience. It is one of those application forms where they walk you through, and you pretty much just give "yes" or "no" answers. How would you suggest getting through the red tape so that I can get my resume to someone with real hiring authority?—Angela Smith

Breaking Through the HR Veil

If there is a place on the form where you can write a note to the recipient, just as you wrote above to me, telling him/her that you would like to have an address to email your special qualifications and capabilities, maybe they would respond. If there is any name, address, phone number either on the form or on the company website that you can communicate with, do so. Sometimes the company website, that uses the online form, has a "contact us" email address, snail mail address, or phone number, you can communicate with them that way.

Search for Points of Contact Other Than HR

Research the company's website. Search news articles on the company. Sometimes you may find a name of a person from that company in the articles. Call the company's main phone number and ask the operator to connect you, or ask for the person's mailing address.

Get Insider Help

If you know anyone in the company, get them to place your resume in the right hiring manager's hands. Call company employees at random and strike up a conversation. You may just happen to contact a sociable person who will tell you anything and everything you would ever want to know about the company. Sometimes, they will even send you information that you would never expect to receive. So, network and gain their trust. Then, they well send/give you any information you desire.

Leah Belmonte Reports Success

For the occupational analysis report (OAR), I sent out questionnaires to local people related to the career that I would like to pursue. I am still receiving them back! It is amazing how many people are willing to help out and share some information with a complete stranger.

Not only have I received insider information from them, but I have realized that this is a great way to begin a networking circle. I first contacted them by phone, then sent them the questionnaire via email, and then a thank you note after they completed the questionnaire. Two of the people that filled out my questionnaire are still emailing me and keeping the communication line open. They have also offered to meet personally with me and share more information.

I'm very pleased with the response from our local community. This was a great opportunity for me to reach out and make some connections.

Preparing Effective Resumes

Bullets That Pack a Punch

I am in my current job because I was recruited while working for another company. My current boss came into my work, liked what he saw, and offered me a job on the spot. Should I include this as a bullet on my resume, and if so, do you have ideas on how to pack a punch with that?

Yes and no. Yes, you can create and use a bullet to describe your previous job. No, you should not use this bullet to describe your new job. Since I do not know what you have done on your previous job, I do not know how to create the "feature" for your bullet; however, the "benefit" to this bullet can be the fact that you were "offered a job on the spot." Hence, if, for example, you were the top producer in the company on your previous job, say bringing in revenues of $5,000 a day, then, you can write the bullet as such:

- Sold on average $5,000 of goods per day, impressed a visiting hiring manager, and received a job offer on the spot.

Because I do not know the background of your previous job, I made up the $5,000 of goods per day just to create a "feature" to your bullet. You would need to insert the real facts that motivated your new boss to make you such an offer "on the spot."

For a complete treatise on how to prepare resumes that pack a punch, acquire a copy of my recent book titled *Resumes That Pack a Punch! Creating Beefy Bullets That Grab, Hook, and Wow Hiring Managers into Calling You for an Interview.* You can obtain this book at iUniverse.com, BarnesandNoble.com, Amazon.com, and other bookseller websites.

Including an Honor Society on Resume but with No Participation

When I went to MiraCosta College, I was part of Phi Theta Kappa, an honor society; however, I never attended meetings, so I really couldn't talk too much about it. So, should I list this association on my resume?

If you have room for it on your resume, yes, by all means, list it. It is an honor to be in PTK; so, you might just as well include it. If you are concerned about the interviewer asking questions about it, go to the PTK website and bone up on the organization. You should at least know the organization's purpose and activities. Do not volunteer your activity level in the organization. However, if asked directly as to your participation, do not lie. Tell the truth that you were unable to participate much because of other priorities. Then, move on to the next subject.

Tailoring Your Resume for a Small Niche Retail Shipping Industry

I grew up around a family business within the retail shipping industry. I have worked within this field for over six years, and I feel that I could possibly be a real asset for companies such as UPS, FedEx, and/or DHL. The type of job I am looking for is a sales position that is responsible for managing retail-shipping accounts similar to my family business.

I really feel that I fit into a small niche that understands these types of customers. I was wondering how I could put a positive spin on my resume in regards to promoting my experience in the field for the past six years. Do you have any suggestions as to how I might do this?—Lauren O'Sullivan

You need to create bullets that pack a punch from your past six years of experience in your family business that will support your sales position in your identified retail-shipping niche. Accentuate your relevant transferable skills and experience.

Join a couple of professional selling organizations to help build your resume and get involved in their monthly meetings. Run for office, get elected, and serve in positions and on committees. Take a certification course/program to build more credibility in this area. Get an internship. Do whatever it takes to build up your resume.

Using Standard Templates

For the personal career portfolio (PCP) cover letter, is it appropriate for me to take a generic template cover letter from the Microsoft website and modify it to make it work with the job for which I am applying?—Roman Bogomolny

You Decide What is Best for You

Yes, it is appropriate for you to start with a generic template cover letter from the Microsoft website and modify it to use for your personal career portfolio (PCP) resume cover letter. However, I haven't yet found any template of either a resume or a cover letter that is better than what I can personally do myself as a tailored/customized resume and cover letter. It is up to you, however. You decide what is best for you.

The Only Purpose or Objective of a Resume

Remember, the bottom line of all resumes and cover letters is this: Do they achieve their only objective? And what is their only objective? Of course, to get you calls for interviews. *Remember, both resumes and cover letters are sales/marketing documents.* They must sell and convince the hiring manager to call you in for an interview. Also, remember, every resume you send out should always be accompanied with a cover letter.

> *Remember, both resumes and cover letters are sales/marketing documents.*

Interviewing for the Job

An Abruptly Canceled Pre-scheduled Interview

This past April, I applied for an internship with a big accounting firm in their finance department. I was later contacted and had a telephone interview scheduled. The first interview went well and I was contacted again to have my second interview at the office in downtown San Diego. I was given detailed instructions on what to wear, where to go, and where to park. I even received a confirmation email stating my interview time and location with directions!

Two days before the second interview, I received a phone call stating that there were too many applicants, and that the manager did not want to interview any other applicants. I was shocked and very disappointed. What happened? I wanted to tell them that they were making a huge mistake, but instead I was very understanding and thanked them for calling. What should I have done?

Consider Yourself Very Lucky

You did the right thing. Consider yourself very lucky to have not interviewed and been offered a job with this accounting division, which is, basically, a sweatshop. My son worked for them for over a year. They worked him to death with late nights and weekends of grunting, menial labor. My son was their top recruit that year...so he was told. Obviously, it was just a "come on" just to get him to join their company.

What a Lousy Company!

Since he was on salary, he made a pittance for an hourly rate after figuring in all of the "free" overtime work they had coerced him to do. The heavy overtime work he did was mainly because this firm wanted to bill their customers with many unnecessary, make-work hours. I am told that of all divisions of this firm, this division is the worst for overtime work. What a lousy company!

There are Better Companies

On the other hand, whenever I work the exorbitant hours of free overtime that I normally do, I do it on my own volition. That's the big difference. I work free overtime because I want to; whereas, he worked much unpaid overtime because he had to so they could bill their customers for the overtime hours. What a rip off! After working there for over a year, my son found a much better company to work for with very little free overtime work…only when it is required to meet hard deadlines.

Don't Work for an Inferior Firm

The stunt that this firm pulled on you is only another indicator that they are a shoddy, inferior house. They are disorganized and don't know what they are doing. They hire people only to serve as indentured servants. They would work you until either you quit or they burn you out…then they would fire you. What kind of company is that! Would you really want to work for such a lousy bunch?

Life is Too Short to Work for Such Companies

There are many other companies just like them. Your job is to find them, weed them off your list of companies to work for, and find those companies that treat their employees as human beings and assets instead of just slaves. Life is too short to work for companies like that. You are fortunate that it ended that way. If not, you would have gone to work for them and ended the same way my son did…leaving after a year. Consider yourself fortunate.

Foot in the Door

I read about a receiving position at Sears. I applied for that position through the Internet. However, when I went to the interview, the interviewer said that receiving position was already filled. Instead, she offered me another position called merchandize customer assistance (MCA). I accepted that position because I thought the MCA position would give me an opportunity to explore the company in other areas. I feel that I do not benefit from this position. What could I have done in this situation?

Your Attitude is Key to Your Success

You could have rejected the position, but then you wouldn't have found out what the MCA position was all about. You would have wondered about it forever. By the way, why are you so hung up on the receiving position? If you took the receiving position, you may have also found out that it wasn't all what you thought it was cracked up to be. On the other hand, you could take the MCA position and expand it into something big, Big, BIG! It's all about your attitude.

The Interviewer Must Have Felt Guilty and Sorry

You were actually fortunate to have been offered the MCA position after they had already filled the receiving position. *There are no guarantees in life.* The interviewer must have felt guilty and sorry for offering the receiving position to another person without giving you an opportunity to interview for it first. So, your being offered the MCA position was a slam dunk. As I said earlier, you could have turned it down, or you could have negotiated it to the hilt and got a lot more out of it than otherwise.

You Have an "Edge" on Others

You expressed regret that you had thought the MCA position would give you an opportunity to explore the company in other areas. It does give you that opportunity! You are now inside the company; whereas, there are many people outside the company that would give at least an arm if not a leg also to be inside looking around for better positions. You are in a very advantageous position to find out about other opportunities. You have an "edge" on others.

Do the Best Job You Can While in This Position

However, if you are to receive any other opportunities within the company, you must do an outstanding job at your current position. If you are not the best MCA in the company, why would the company offer you a better position within the company? If you don't do superbly at your MCA position, you might just as well get out of there and find another job. If you are not doing fantastically as an MCA, that position will not help your resume look better. In fact, it could hurt you if you cannot put down a couple of bullets that "pack a punch."

Turn All Negatives Into Positives

So, the moral of the story is you should make the best of your MCA position so that it will help you capture a better job on your next go-around. Don't let this bad job make your resume look worse. Turn a negative thing into a positive by doing your best to create a couple of bullets that will make an impact on getting a better

> *There is a silver lining in every dark cloud.*

position on your next job search. Do you understand what I am saying here?

There is a silver lining in every dark cloud. Find that lining and use it to your advantage instead of it being a setback. Now, go do it!

Would Name Dropping Give You an Advantage?

When applying to a company where you already know somebody that is currently working there, is it appropriate to mention their name during an interview or ask them to call HR and put in a good word for you? While it could be a plus that I might already know somebody at the company, what if HR interviewer does not like that employee?—Roman Bogomolny

Leverage Your Friendships

By all means, yes! It is quite appropriate to drop names. I encourage you to mention the name of people whom you know that work in the company for which you are seeking to be hired. It is a real plus if you are good friends of these people. Take full advantage of that friendship. Email them your latest resume. Ask them to get it into the hiring manager's hands. That is a real advantage. Leverage your friendships. After all, that is only making use of your networking nodes.

Friends Make the Best Kind of Future Employees

In many companies, when employees bring in their friends into the company, they would receive a recruiting bonus of about $1,000 or more depending on the level of the individual. In fact, that is the best kind of people to bring into the company…one's friends. The chance of getting a good employee is much better hiring friends than hiring someone from the outside that they know nothing about and based only on an interview.

You Want Good Employees to Advance Your Candidacy

If an employee you know is not liked by the HR interviewer, that is not a good situation. However, it is not as detrimental as when the hiring manager does not like your employee friend. In that case, you have a real problem. You might distance yourself from such an employee. You want good, solid employee friends to recommend you to hiring managers. Their word must carry weight with hiring managers. You want well-liked people pushing your resume within the companies they work.

Questions to Ask at the End of an Interview

I have a hard time responding to the question…"What questions do you have for me?" at the end of an interview. What type of questions am I suppose to ask?—Alison McCamish

Ask a Question Each on Goals and Strategy

At the end of the interview, when your interviewer asks you if you have any questions, ask him/her a question regarding the company's goals. Then ask a question regarding the company's strategy to achieve their goals. So, these questions can be as follows:

Question #1: Would you give me a general idea of your major goals for this organization over the next three to five years?

Question #2: Would you tell me about your overall strategy for accomplishing those goals?

The All-Important Question to Ask at the End of the Interview

This is the most important secret: Then, finally, looking the interviewer eyeball-to-eyeball, without any flinching, ask this question:

Question #3: Now that you have read my resume and have interviewed me, from everything that I have said, do you feel that my background and capabilities meet your requirements (or have a place in your organization)?

Give the Interviewer an Opportunity to Answer

Pause and maintain focused eye contact. Do not ever leave an interview without asking this question. The answer you receive and the manner in which your interviewer answers this question will give you a good clue as to whether or not you will receive an offer.

Know Whether or Not You will Receive an Offer

If the interviewer pauses for a fraction of a second or glances away from your eye contact, you will know that you do not have the offer locked yet. Then, you know you have your work cut out for you in the post-interview period. However, if the interviewer says, "Yes, you are the perfect candidate for the job, and I will be recommending to my management that we hire you," then, you know you will officially receive an offer soon.

Demonstrate Boldness and Assertiveness

In fact, you could even boldly go further. You could ask how many candidates are in serious contention for the position and how you rank within this shortlist. This approach leaves no doubt as to where you stand in the interview ranking. Further, it demonstrates assertiveness on your part, which they typically appreciate.

Know Exactly What You will Do Before You Leave

Upon parting company, ask the interviewer, "Where do we go from here?" He/she should tell you when they will make the final decision and will contact you to let you know whether you will receive the offer. Then, ask the interviewer this question: "If I do not hear from you in a week to 10 days, would it be okay if I called you?" Invariably, the interviewer will say, "Yes." However, if you do not receive a call from the company in 10 days, do not miss calling back to ascertain the status of the decision process. Not calling as promised is self-destructive.

Notes, Cards, Emails, and Business Cards

I have a few questions for you. Sending a thank you note after being interviewed is considered to be a smart move. I know that many corporations, such as the one at which I presently work, conduct a series of interviews before hiring. When I interviewed for a position, it was two days of interviews, and with each interview, you gradually climb up the totem pole. It went as follows:

- *HR hiring manager*
- *Assistant department manager*
- *Department manager*
- *Rooms division manager*
- *Hotel manager*

I was hired without the final interview by the hotel manager, but you get what I'm saying. So my question is this: Who do you send the thank you note to after the interview process is complete? My other question to you is this: In your book, you say that when we go to career fairs and things of that nature, we should hand out business cards. You suggest that we get some if we don't have them already. What should they say on them as the title? PBS?

More and More a Battery of Interviews is the Norm

Yes, most large corporations have a battery of interviews where you go either serially through about a half-dozen interviewers or in a group or panel interview.

They are usually exhausting and intimidating. When I had interviewed with Titan Wireless, I had to go through three separate days of interviews because they couldn't gather all of the required people on the same day as several were frequent business travelers.

Always Send a Thank You Note

Yes, always send a thank you card, note, or email after an interview. More and more, a well-written email is just as effective as a card or note sent by snail mail. Personally, I prefer an email from the people I interview. It gets to me faster and I can see how much effort they put into it by the typos, misspelled words, and punctuation errors they have on it if they did it in a "quick and dirty" fashion. Send your thank you communication within 24 hours of the interview.

How to Send Thank You Correspondence

When you send thank you cards, notes, or email, the best approach would be to send them to each person with whom you interviewed. If you send an email, you can send the same email to all of them. If there is a reason to send separate emails, then do so.

Panel Interview Need Only One Email

When I had interviewed with the Defense Acquisition University (DAU), it was a panel interview. Hence, I sent the same email (with everyone on distribution) to all five members of the panel including the person who was piped in by video teleconferencing (VTC) from another part of the country. I also Cc'd the dean, which proved to be a good move for me.

Don't Leave Out Anyone That Could Help

However, I also sent a special email to the administrative assistant (a college student who was interning there) who had picked me up at the gate and returned me to the gate after the interview. She was so impressed with my thank you note that she sent a very nice reply email back to me. No telling how many people she either told about my nice email to her or forwarded my email to them.

Follow-up Emails Can Really Help

A day later, I also sent a separate email to one of the panel interviewers because he had expressed interest in knowing what uniform resource locator (URL) at which (at that time) my seven published books were shown. So, I sent the URLs of all of my books to him, which was a good move on my part.

I also communicated frequently with this individual because I noticed during and after the interview that he had taken a special liking of me. We communicated by back-and-forth email as though we were good buddies! So, I capitalized on that advantage and leveraged it to my greater advantage. Can you see how effective well-placed emails can be?

Free Business Cards

Yes, when you attend networking events, job fairs, and interviews, you should hand out business cards. You can obtain free business cards from http://www.vistaprint.com. You get 250 cards free because they place a small advertisement on the back of each card. You only need to pay for the shipping cost, which comes to about four to five dollars.

Always Have a Title

If you are unemployed, you probably won't have a title. If you are a graduating student, you can use that as a title. Everyone should have their own sole proprietorship (small business) so that you can use a title as president, business owner, founder, general manager, consultant, or whatever you want to call yourself.

Personal Brand Statement

You could also include your personal brand statement (PBS) on the card. However, you can cut it down to just a few words. The 15-word requirement was just for an academic exercise in our class. So, streamline your PBS to one that is concise and effective. For examples of PBSs, refer to Appendix A of this book.

Dealing with Unfulfilled Promises Made During the Interview Process

If certain promises were made to you during the interview process and after several months of working for a firm those promises have not been delivered, how and when should you approach your boss?

Confront Your Boss if Promises Were Not Kept

You should approach your boss about this problem sooner rather than later. Straight out state to him or her that, during the interview, he/she had made certain unfulfilled promises to you. Then, delineate those promises to establish agreement. If your boss disagrees, then you both need to discuss it to come to some kind of agreement.

Either Stay and Stop Stewing or Quit

If you are positive of the promises made to you but not kept and he/she will not make good on them, then you have a decision to make, i.e., you should either stay or quit. If the job is good enough to endure it for a year, stay. If the job is not that good, find another job, quit, and move on. It is as simple as that. It is not good for your health to stew about promises you feel have been made but not kept.

Always Get Agreements in Writing

This is why it is always prudent to have all pre-employment agreements documented in the offer letter. *Always put agreements down in writing*. Never expect anyone to keep verbal pre-employment promises. Always, always, always get them down in writing. Then, the agreements become legal agreements that will stand up in court.

> *Always put agreements down in writing.*

There May Be Misunderstandings

I once hired a woman who wanted to take a prearranged two-week trip to Europe only two weeks after she started working for me. During the interview, I agreed to allow her to take the time off from work even though she had accumulated but a miniscule amount of vacation time. Never did I state that it would be a paid two-week leave. The company had a policy that said nobody could take leave without the required accumulated, earned vacation time.

It Could Be a Fabrication

After her two-week trip to Europe, she approached me stating that I had agreed in the interview to give her a two-week paid vacation. I was positive that I had made no such agreement because company policy did not allow me to do that, and I had told her so. Her fabricating such a story after I had let her go on vacation shortly after starting work made me quite angry.

I was Willing to Let Her Quit

However, she realized that I had really bent over backwards to allow her to take a two-week unpaid leave after starting work on her new job just a mere two weeks earlier. Hence, she stayed. However, her taking advantage of my kindness to let her take off for two weeks only after being on the job for a mere two weeks, I was willing to let her quit…and almost encouraged it.

Two Sides to Every Story

Remember, there are always two sides to every story. To get any kind of mutually successful resolution to any disagreement, both parties must agree to whatever is in contention. Just be sure that you are positive about your side of the story before bringing anything to a head.

Brag Book—How to Improve Your PCP

In starting to work on my Personal Career Portfolio (PCP), I've found that I do not really have any awards to show. Is it too late to try to achieve an award or do volunteer work to try to make my PCP better since I am almost done with college. Also, would it be helpful or look good to volunteer at a hospital and put that in my PCP even though it is not the field I want to go into?

Pursue All Possible Awards

It is never too late to improve your PCP whether it is winning awards or serving as a volunteer in many civic/service organizations. If you have no awards to show, you need to start now to win awards. A good place you could have started on was to win at least one of the 20+ awards that I had presented at the end of the semester.

Do Whatever It Takes to Improve Your PCP and Resume

It is never too late to achieve an award or to do volunteer work to try to make your PCP look better. Any kind of volunteer work (especially in a hospital) will help your PCP look better. You should also join several professional organizations and take additional schooling perhaps to get a certification. Get involved in your professional organizations. All of these activities would help improve both your PCP and resume.

Awards Don't Just Fall into Your Lap

At my new job at work, over 25 awards are presented at the end of each fiscal year. Guess what? I have my eye on a few of them for next year. If you don't set goals for any awards, you will never win them. Good awards don't just fall into your lap. You must plan for them, pursue them, politic for them, and then win them. It all doesn't occur just by happenstance.

To the Victors Go the Spoils

If you don't seek after them, you will not win them. So, go after the awards you want to win. Then, you'll be able to write better bullets on your resume and improve the quality and thickness of your PCP. Only to the victors go the spoils of war. You must win the battle to win the prize. Go for it!

Negotiating to Win

Effective Salary Negotiations

When is the proper time to negotiate what you believe to be a fair salary and what are good ways of going about this without sounding money hungry? Upon going into the interview, if you are unsure about what the salary is going to be, how do you go about finding this out?

Two Appropriate Times to Negotiate Your Salary

There are two appropriate times to negotiate your salary. The *first time* is when and if the hiring manager brings up salary during your interviews. *Do not ever bring up salary before your interviewer brings it up.* When the interviewer broaches the subject, ask him/her if he/she is making you an offer. If he/she is, then you can talk/negotiate your salary. If he/she says, "no," he/she is not making you an offer, then, say you will be happy to discuss salary when he/she is prepared to make you an offer. The *second time*

> *Do not ever bring up salary before your interviewer brings it up.*

that would be appropriate to negotiate salary is when you receive an offer letter. Then, negotiate to the hilt but in a nice manner, of course.

Do Your Homework

If you are unsure about what your salary should be, you can get a better handle of it by doing the following:

- *Research.* Perform salary research on the Internet. You can find many salary websites by going to "Ask Jeeves at http://www.ask.com." Find out what salaries newly minted graduates in similar career fields receive.
- *Analyze.* Determine what bare minimum salary you will accept and what you really want for a salary. These two extremes comprise the range of your salary requirements. However, what you are really worth is what you accept, and that would be your lowest threshold figure.
- *Negotiate.* When the hiring company initiates salary discussion, they will ask you for your salary history and your desired salary range. When they

ask you for these, ask them what salary range they have for this job. You need to get an idea of their salary range that they are willing to offer you. The mid-point of that range is usually where they want to end up.

Know Exactly What You are Going to Do

If you have done sufficient homework and are well prepared, you can conduct effective salary negotiations. Never go into salary negotiations not know knowing exactly:

- What salary they will offer you
- What salary range they are willing to give you
- What salary others of similar background and education are receiving
- What salary you want
- What salary you will accept and receive
- What salary you are worth, which is exactly what you will accept

If you know all of these things, you will not risk leaving any money on the negotiating table.

Dealing with Salary History

Upon sending in my resume to a company and being called in for an interview, how do I omit including past earnings in the job application? Is it acceptable to write on the application "Will be discussed during the interview"?—Catalina Garcia

Do Not Give Your Salary History Before the Interview

You do not want to give your salary history before you receive an interview. This is because companies use salary histories to weed out highly-paid candidates. Some companies also use this information to determine the salary ranges of all people in your area doing similar work. This knowledge helps them maintain the "upper hand" in salary negotiations with you.

Get Them to Pay You What You are Worth

Once you get in for an interview, then it is okay to reveal your salary history only when they are ready to make you an offer. When you interview, you have an opportunity to prove to the interviewers that you are worth the high salary you command. Once the hiring manager is impressed with you, a high

> *Whatever you are worth is what you will accept.*

salary is not as much of a problem. If you are in great demand, the hiring company will pay you whatever you are worth. *Remember, whatever you are worth is what you will accept.*

Filling Out the Application Forms

When I know a company wants me badly enough, I do not fill out the application before I go in for the interview. When they ask for it in the interview, I tell them that I will type it out ASAP and get it to them post haste. They are usually receptive to this approach. Of course, if they were not hotly pursuing me, they would use my not completing and submitting the application as their reason for discontinuing any more discussions. Oh, well!

How Do You Negotiate a Better Offer if Pay Scales are Pre-established?

How would you negotiate an offer if the company bases salary on your experience and do not offer perks as you mentioned in class. I work for a college where the pay scale is already set up and depends on experience. Any suggestions especially if you feel that you can do the job that is available but don't have the experience.—Eva Viveros

Life is Too Short to Work for Inflexible Organizations

I don't know of any company or establishment that you cannot negotiate anything. Yes, some governmental organizations have set pay scales. However, there are many kinds of perquisites (perks) that can be negotiated. If they give you absolutely no room for salary or perks negotiations, then, perhaps, you should find an organization that provides you with some room for negotiations. There are too many good organizations out there that you do not need to be forced to limit yourself only to just one…the one that will not negotiate anything. Life is too short for that.

Develop Your Own Leverage

If you have no experience in the job you want to get into, then you need to take preparatory jobs that will give you that experience. You can also get an advanced degree and specialize in that new career area. Furthermore, you can complete a certification program in that new job area. Join professional organizations in the career field you seek to enter. Participate in the local chapter of these organizations. More than one way exists to acquire the education and experience needed to get into your passion job. You need to find those ways to prepare yourself for what you desire.

How to Find Out About Prevailing Salaries

What is the best way to find out what your peers are being paid and/or what a competitive wage/salary is for your industry?—Matt Martinez

Get the Book!

Note: I already answered this question in my book titled *Career Quest for College Graduates*, chapter 6, page 87, on "Salary." Get the book!

Go to Ask Jeeves and Do Some Research

Go to Ask Jeeves at http://www.ask.com and do some research on entry-level salaries for the job you seek. Find out what the going rate is in the location that you desire to work. Through your research, you should be able to determine the range of salaries for entry-level jobs in the discipline you are in and for the location in which you will be working.

Establish Your Desired Personal Salary Range

Then, determine exactly what you desire for a salary and what the lowest salary amount below which you absolutely cannot and will not go. These two figures give you your personal salary range that you desire.

Compare Your Desires to Prevailing Industry Ranges

Now, compare the prevailing industry salary range against your personal salary range. If they coincide or have a range of overlap, you are in good shape. If your personal range is below the industry range with no overlap whatsoever, you need to have an attitude adjustment. Chances are you have a very low self-image and self-esteem.

Adjust Your Desires to the Prevailing Industry Range

On the other hand, if your personal range is above the industry range with no overlap at all, that indicates that either you have no concept of reality or you have an over-inflated ego and think you are worth much more than you are actually worth. Again, you need an attitude adjustment. Lower your personal range to have some overlap with the industry range.

Terri Levine Writes

Terri Levine, president of Comprehensive Coaching U, in an article in *The Wall Street Journal* titled "The Top 7 Signs of Self-Sabotaging Behaviors," lists seven signs of self-sabotaging behaviors as follows:

1. Focusing on what is not working or not right
2. Being stuck in fear
3. Feeling you have no value
4. Comparison of self to others
5. Meeting goals and then losing them
6. You chase away relationships
7. Having no purpose[6]

Develop a Personal Mission in Life and Pursue Your Passions

You must not wallow in these counterproductive behaviors. Instead, focus on what is working and right. Work on your self-confidence. Learn to like yourself and feel that you are worth a lot. Refrain from comparing yourself to those who are way above-and-beyond you. As you accomplish goals (no matter how small they are), relish in those little victories. Work on your network and cultivate good, meaningful relationships. Above all, develop goals and a plan to accomplish them. Develop a personal mission in life and pursue your passions.

You are Worth Exactly What You Accept

Now, all of this discussion is fine and dandy. That's ivory tower talk. However, *what you are really worth is what you accept, or you are worth exactly what you accept, or you are only worth what you accept.* That's getting down to reality. If you accept anything below the industry range, that's what you are worth. Worse yet, if you actually accept a salary below what you had set as your lowest limit in your personal salary range, that's all you are worth, which is worse than worst! You probably will be living in poverty.

> *Develop a personal mission in life and pursue your passions.*

Don't Accept a Salary Below the Poverty Level

Don't live in poverty. The average poverty figure in the United States is $30,000 or below per year of gross income. Do not accept anything below the poverty level. Why do you go to college and graduate if you will accept a poverty salary level? Trade workers will be making more than you would be making.

---

6. Terri Levine, President, Comprehensive Coaching U—as seen in *The Wall Street Journal* is the author of bestseller, *Work Yourself Happy & Coaching for an Extraordinary Life.* www.coachinginstruction.com.

College graduates should make more money than do blue-collar workers. Don't insult yourself, your college, and all college graduates by accepting a poverty level salary. Expect the best and get it!

> *The average poverty figure in the United States is $30,000 or below per year of gross income.*

Seek to Receive the Industry Average or Better

The National Association of Colleges and Employers (NACE) prepared the data in the following table, which indicates what a degree is worth and what are starting salaries for the class of 2005.

WHAT'S A DEGREE WORTH?
Here are some average starting salaries for the class of 2005:

MAJOR	STARTING	VS. 2004
Chemical engineering	$54,256	+4.3%
Electrical engineering	$52,009	+2.5%
Computer engineering	$51,496	-2.0%
Computer science	$51,292	+2.6%
Mechanical engineering	$51,046	+4.1%
Aerospace engineering*	$50,701	+9.0%
Industrial Engineering	$49,541	+1.8%
Accounting	$43,809	+3.9%
Information sciences	$43,732	-0.8%
Civil engineering	$43,462	+4.0%
Economics/finance	$42,802	+5.1%
Business administration	$39,448	+3.2%
Marketing	$37,832	+6.0%
Liberal arts	$30,337	+4.2%

Source:
National Association of Colleges and Employers
*Also aeronautical and astronautical engineering degrees

Do Not Go Below the Poverty Level!

All business graduates should be able to earn an annual starting salary between $30,000 to $44,000. The average student should easily be able to receive $36,000 per annum. If you accept less, that's what you're really worth, no more. Remember, if you take below $30,000 per annum, you will be receiving a poverty-level salary, so do not go below $30,000 per annum!

Strive to Be a Person Who "Walks on Water"

If you are an average student, you should be able to obtain $36,000–$40,000 per annum. The average BSBA graduate should be able to obtain $39,500 per annum. If you are a super student, you should be able to get between $40,000–$44,000 per annum. If you walk on water, you should be able to get over $44,000 per annum.

Maximize Your Starting Salary!

As usual, engineering and computer science graduates will receive the most money ($49,000–$55,000 per annum!), which can be over $10,000 per year more than highest paid business and finance graduates. Hence, it pays to work hard to pass all of those math, physics, chemistry, engineering, and computer science courses. Now, go out there and maximize your starting salary by proving your worth and negotiating to the hilt!

> *Any business graduate should be able to garner between $30,000–$40,000 annual starting salary.*

Another Cut of the Survey

"Employers tell us that the economy is improving, and likewise, more positions are open for new college graduates," explains Andrea J. Koncz, NACE's Employment Information Manager. Majors topping the list also boast significant annual earnings boosts—accounting ($44,564), management trainee ($35,811), software design and development ($53,729), and design/construction engineering ($47,048).[7] These average salary levels provide tremendous opportunities for college graduates this year. Remember, do not accept an annual salary below $30,000.

---

7.   AOL Research & Learn: Online Campus—"Need a Job? Good News—Prospects and Paychecks Increase," article by Gina LaGuardia, 2005-04-21 12:11:02.

Top 10 Jobs for 2004–05 Graduates

Job Function	Average Salary Offer
Software Design & Development	$53,729
Consulting	$49,781
Design/Construction Engineering	$47,058
Financial/Treasury Analysis	$45,596
Accounting (Private)	$44,564
Accounting (Public)	$41,039
Sales	$37,130
Management Trainee (Entry-Level Mgmt.)	$35,811
Teaching	$29,733

Source: Spring 2005 Salary Survey, National Association of Colleges & Employers (NACE). All data is for bachelor's degree candidates. Rankings are based on number of offers reported.

Negotiating a Vacation during the Hiring Process

Is it unprofessional to negotiate a vacation in the hiring process?

No, it is not unprofessional and it is okay to negotiate a vacation during the hiring process. However, you should have a compelling reason to negotiate such a vacation during the hiring process. The hiring manager must want very much for you to come to work for them. In this situation, you possess what is called *leverage*. However, if the hiring manager has other equally qualified, potential candidates ready to assume the job you are seeking, then you do not possess enough leverage to attempt to negotiate successfully a vacation during the hiring process.

How Would I Know That an Out-of-State Job is a Good One?

I may have a potential job offer as a marketing manager after graduation. It would be a fantastic opportunity, but it would require me to work in Arizona. If the money and experience are acceptable, I would definitely move. From everything that I have heard, it sounds like a great job. How do I go about asking what level is the salary? In the meantime, should I also continue to look into internships and other job opportunities? What if, during the time before graduation, I find another opportunity? How would I tell the current potential job offeror that I have decided to work for another company and still be able to encourage them to keep me in mind in the future?

Salary Discussion

If you are that far along on landing this job, I'm surprised that the salary subject hasn't yet been broached by the hiring company. By now, they should have asked you for your desired salary range and your salary history. If they make you an offer, then you can point-blank ask them what salary comes with the job.

Moving to Arizona

If they hire you for this marketing manager position, take it and move to Arizona. Arizona is not that bad of a place to live. Granted, not many places can beat San Diego County. However, the Phoenix area is growing by leaps-and-bounds. Apparently, many people have uprooted their families and moved to Arizona, which indicates that it is a desirable place to live and work. You are young and do not have too many responsibilities to keep you tied to San Diego. If you find that the job is not that great, you can always move back to Southern California in a year or so.

Keep Your Job Searching Effort Going

In the meantime, you should continue your job searching effort. Never stop your effort until you have a written offer-in-hand, and you have accepted the offer. Even then, sometimes, hiring companies retract offers before you start working for them. Hence, it is a good idea to keep your job searching effort going until you actually start working for that company. Then, you can quit searching.

Keep Your Options Open

If you accept an offer and then, later, you receive an even better offer, take the better offer, run, and never look back. Just write the first company a nice letter and tell them that you had another offer that you just could not refuse. However, forget about ever going back to that company to work for them in the future. There are enough companies out there that you don't need to be focused on only one company. So, don't worry about it. Move forward, onward, and upward.

Go Forward!

Bank of America (BOA) was on campus today and I spoke to the recruiter. I told him that I was recently offered a position as a teller but I had to decline it due to another offer from Washington Mutual (WaMu). He asked how much they offered me, but I did not want to disclose that amount. Is he allowed to ask me that? I told him how much more they offered which, basically, tells them what my offer was.

He then asked me which recruiters I spoke with, and I told him who they were. He knew both of them. He asked what part of town I live in, and then he mentioned that there was an opening nearby. I told him where my position would be, and then he immediately knew who the manager was. He asked for my contact information, and he said that he will talk to the recruiter and the district manager to see what they can do.

I am interested in BOA, but not as much anymore since I got the job from WaMu. If I get a better offer, should I take it? I start this Thursday at WaMu. A friend referred me to WaMu, so I don't want to back out at the last minute. Recently, I have debated if I should have taken the BOA offer since they have tuition reimbursement, and they will pay for licenses for series 6, 7, and so on. He said that they will contact me, or he will call me personally to see what they can do. I asked for his business card, and I thanked him for his time.

Keep Them Guessing

On your first question, "Is he allowed to ask me that?," the answer is "yes." He can ask you anything he desires. This is a free country, so he can ask you anything. However, that does not mean that you need to answer the question or give him the amount WaMu offered you.

What he wanted was the amount you will make so that he can come back with a counteroffer at a slightly higher amount that you will be receiving from WaMu. What you should have said is this: "I am not disclosing what WaMu had offered me, but it was much more than what BOA had offered me." Keep him guessing. Do not ever give them the amount you were offered.

Do Not Prostitute Yourself

On your second question: "If I get a better offer, should I take it?" Your question indicates that you are willing to prostitute yourself. You have already proven that, and now it all depends on the dollars they are willing to pay you. I am certain you have a price that would coax you away from the WaMu offer.

Much of Leveraging is Perception

Here is the problem you will get yourself into should you prostitute yourself. Because you had turned down BOA for WaMu, they feel rejected and unhappy that you did not go with them. Now, when they wave a few more dollars in front of your eyes and you take it, they know you are a prostitute and, therefore, they will dislike you even more.

However, when you go to work for them, you will have lost your leveraging capability and will now be under their control. *Remember, much of leveraging is perception.* Because you have proven yourself as a prostitute to them, they will not treat you as well as they would have had you accepted their first offer over WaMu. Do you see the dynamics here?

> *Remember, much of leveraging is perception.*

Know the Dynamics Involved with Negotiations

When you withdraw your acceptance of the WaMu offer, you will make them unhappy by appearing to prostitute yourself. Should they increase their offer to beat the new BOA offer and you decide to stay with them, they will then have you under their control. However, they will feel differently about you because you showed yourself as a figurative prostitute. Do you see the dynamics involved here?

Negotiate Aggressively on the First Go-around

So, how do you avoid appearing as a prostitute by both BOA and WaMu, yet negotiate successfully? You do this by applying your leveraging and negotiating strategies to the hilt on the first go-around. If you recall, you did not negotiate to the hilt on the first go-around. Instead, once BOA said they would not increase their offer, you then accepted the WaMu offer. You could have aggressively negotiated with WaMu to get them to increase their offer or even negotiated other benefits such as getting them to pay tuition assistance for your master's program. As we recall, however, you did not do that. Hence, you missed an opportunity to sweeten the WaMu deal.

Re-negotiating Your Salary Puts You in a Very Precarious Position

By attempting to re-negotiate now after the company deals are closed, you put yourself in a very precarious position, i.e., appearing as a figurative prostitute. No matter what company you go with now, by attempting to reopen negotiations, you end up looking bad in both companies' eyes. Do you understand the situation in which you find yourself?

Avoid "Buyer's Remorse" and Appearing Wishy-washy

Whenever you make a decision, you should take it and not look backwards. Do not entertain "buyer's remorse." Take the first decision you make and move forward. By being indecisive at this point, you just appear wishy-washy. Both BOA and WaMu will see that flaw in your character. Instead, go forward.

Move onward and upward. Do not entertain "buyer's remorse." If you now "change
horses in the middle of the stream" and
appear wishy-washy, you will repeat that
shortcoming throughout your life. Instead,
go forward!

> *Do not entertain*
> *"buyer's remorse."*

7

Performance, Raises, and Promotions

FACT: The biggest raises come from salary negotiations when choosing to move on to a NEW employer. Internal raises rarely exceed 5–8% but major increases—20%, 40%, even 50%,—come from selling yourself more effectively to a new company. New employers are offering top dollar just to insure you'll join their team, but ONLY if you know the secrets of salary negotiations. So if your employer isn't paying the true value of what you provide working for them, now is a good time to explore landing a new job with a much higher salary. But avoid committing salary negotiations suicide—do not break this rule: Never reveal your previous salary. Do learn how to effectively sell yourself and know your worth.[8]

Robin Ryan
Career Counselor

To receive raises and promotions, you must be a producer. Just punching in on the time clock, working eight hours, and then punching out on the time clock will not hack it. You must do whatever is necessary to bring in money to your company and help the company flourish, progress, and increase in value. You must be a value adder. You must be a superior performer and produce outstanding results before you will be considered qualified to receive raises and promotions.

---

8. Robin Ryan, "Want a Raise? Don't Commit Salary Suicide," Net-Temps, Inc., Copyright 1995–2006, http://www.net-temps.com/careerdev/crossroads/print.htm?id=1771. America's most popular career counselor, Robin Ryan, is the author of four best-selling books. Contact her at 425-226-0414; email: info@robinryan.com.

Job Performance at a New Job

I have heard from numerous sources that you should arrive early and stay late in order to establish yourself as a hard worker at the company. I agree that it is a good idea, but how do you avoid looking like you're trying to upstage your manager if you are not able to see the general manager often?—Heather Murphy

The Security of Your Manager is Important to Know

Good question! If you work for an insecure manager, always leave just before or at the same time he/she leaves. Always arrive after he/she arrives. If you work for a "go-getter" manager, you have no worries. If that manager is secure within himself/herself, you have nothing to worry about if you arrive early or leave late.

Never Appear to Upstage Your Manager

Yes, never appear to upstage your manager whether he/she is secure or otherwise. Upstaging your manager in any way is career limiting. If you work for an insecure manager, take your work home with you and get those extra hours of work done without your manager knowing about it. What your manager does not know, doesn't hurt.

Give Your Manager Credit for Your Work

One way to get your manager's support on everything you produce is to put his/her name on the document. If you give your manager credit for the work, he/she will like you. When the time for dishing out the goodies arrives, your manager will most likely give you your fair share of the goodies.

Reaching the Top of the Corporate Mountain

What strategic moves do I need to make to reach the top of the mountain where the corporate executives are found? From the education side, I will obtain an MBA and an MS in finance.—Rigo Ortiz

A Five-point Strategy

Here is my five-point strategy for reaching the top of the corporate mountain:

1. *Relationships.* Network and establish alliances. Establish mentor-protégé relationships. Be totally responsive to your supervisors. Be a person of impeccable integrity. In the leaders over you, develop their total trust in you. Be humble.

2. *Knowledge & Education.* Prepare yourself educationally. In addition to obtaining an MBA and an MS in finance, also think about earning the PhD degree. Be the focal point of all information. *Knowledge is power.* Learn how to speak well and write well. Continue to study throughout your entire career and life. Publish papers and books. Make presentations at conferences.

3. *Good Work Ethic.* Work hard and smart. Strive to be the "best of the best" in an area of specialty within the finance field. Those who make big bucks, hold the most power, and make it to the top are involved in mergers and acquisitions (M's & A's), venture capital (VC), and investments. Build the company. Be a mover and shaker. Make a difference. Add value. Make things happen.

4. *Political Savvy.* Play good politics and be the best at it. Find people you can trust implicitly. Form coalitions. *Always do the right things as well as doing things right.* Always know what is going on behind the scenes. Be visible.

5. *People Treatment.* Think about your people. Help them to be successful, and they will help you to become successful. Develop the support, love, and respect of your direct reports and subordinates. Reward good work. Publicly praise those for which you have stewardship over when they do good work. Be a good listener.

> *Always do the right things as well as doing things right.*

That's it. Implement these five strategic moves in your career, and you will make it to the top. Good luck!

Job Advancement

I currently work for a small company. I have recently been offered a new position in that company that would broaden my skill set. My question is this: Should I accept the position and gain the experience knowing that I will not be staying with the company after I graduate (in three months)?

Take the new position, learn all you can while you serve in it, and leave after you graduate. Don't look back. Your boss must know that you will be leaving after you graduate. This is the reason why your boss has offered you this new position...to try to entice you to stay. However, don't ever feel obligated to stay just because you were offered this new position. You need to go on to bigger-and-better things. So, don't feel guilty about it. Move forward, onward, and upward!

How to Get Into a Corporate Job at Nordstrom

I have been an assistant manager for five years now at a female retail clothing company. I am hoping to get into a corporate position for Nordstrom when I graduate, but they only promote from within. Do you think it is a good idea to step down as an assistant manager and into a sales associate position at Nordstrom so I can eventually move up into a corporate position? I do not know how long it would take until they move me up at Nordstrom. I know at my current job, it may never happen.

Should I continue working at my current job as an assistant manager? Should I look for other management positions since I do have many years of management? Or should I step down as an assistant manager and into a sales associate position at Nordstrom, and hope I will be moved up into the current position I am in now and then eventually into a corporate job at Nordstrom?

Learn the Ropes from Bottom-Up

If you will be staying at Nordstrom for a long time (say 5 to 10 years or more), then I say take the sales associate job. However, if you're the type of person like me (who never seem to stay with the same company for a long time), then you probably should not take the job at Nordstrom. Remember, for a large company like Nordstrom, to get into corporate, you should start at the bottom or close to it. That way, you will learn the ropes from the bottom-up.

Long Trek to the Corporate Office in Large Corporations

In large corporations, it takes a much longer time for young employees to progress into the corporate office. You usually need to have connections at the top or are such a super-producer that top management notices you quickly. Then, you would need to be a very compelling candidate for top management to "take you under their wings" so to speak. I can see why Nordstrom promotes from within. They want their good employees to stick with them for the long haul.

You are Loyal to the Workplace

I see on your Career Success Map Questionnaire (CSMQ) that you have an average 8 on both "getting ahead" and "getting high." However, 8 is your high score, so you don't have a very strong intensity level on any of the five orientations. On your Myers-Briggs Type Indicator (MBTI) or Jung Typology Test (JTT), you are an ESTJ. That says you are extroverted thinking with sensing. Further, you are or will be a responsible mate and parent and loyal to the workplace. You are also realistic, down-to-earth, orderly, and love tradition. You will often find yourself joining civic clubs!

Nordstrom is a Good Place to Work

So, it seems to me that Nordstrom or a company like Nordstrom would be a good place for you to work. If you've worked for five years as an assistant manager, you've already worked in that job two years too long. You need to get into a manager's position on your next job…unless, of course, you go to work for a large corporation like Nordstrom…then you would need to start over from the bottom or close to it.

How to Ask for a Raise

What is the best way to talk to your supervisor regarding your salary and getting a raise?—Matt Martinez

Get the Book!

Note: I already answered this question in my book titled *Career Quest for College Graduates*, chapter 21, page 273, on "Raises." Get the book!

Asking for a Raise

The most appropriate way to ask for a raise is to go into your supervisor's office, sit down, and face-to-face ask him/her for a raise. The worse he/she can do is to say "no." He/she won't kill you. Asking eyeball-to-eyeball is more effective than sending him/her an email or calling by phone. When you ask face-to-face, you can watch your supervisor's eyes and body language. The answer will most likely be "no," but the eyes and body language will clue you in to determine if you will ever receive a raise.

Ask and Ye Shall Receive

Asking also instills in your supervisor's mind that he/she will probably need to consider giving you a raise the next time it is possible, particularly if you are doing outstanding work. If you don't ask, your supervisor may think you are happy with the current situation. By asking, that makes your supervisor aware that you expect something for your good work. That's the key. *If you are not doing good work, forget about getting a raise.* Only if you are doing superior work would you possess sufficient advantage to shake loose a raise in the near or distant future. So, ask and ye shall receive.

> *If you are not doing good work, forget about getting a raise.*

If You are an Average Producer, Forget About Asking

As I said before, there is no better way to ask for a raise than to point-blank ask your boss for that raise. However, you had better possess a lot of leverage when you ask for that raise. In other words, you had better be the best producing direct report of all those who report to him/her. *If you are an average producer, forget about asking for a raise.* He/she would probably laugh you out of his/her office.

> *If you are an average producer, forget about asking for a raise.*

Timing of Asking for a Raise

The best time to ask for a raise is when your supervisor is in a good mood because you were the primary person responsible for capturing a $10 million contract that day. When the moment is right, pop your supervisor the question. For example, you could say, "John, since I was instrumental in bringing in this $10 million contract, would it be appropriate for me to receive a good raise to reward me for my efforts?" Then, look your supervisor straight in the eyes and wait for the answer. Do not say another word. Just wait for the answer.

If Rejected Outright, Look for a Better Company

John will probably say, "I'll see what I can do." That's the best way to do it. Company management would be stupid to turn you down flat. If they reject you immediately upon your asking, start looking for a better company for which to work. Your management would be a bunch of losers to turn you down flat. If they cannot give you a raise, they can give you something else to appease you. For example, they can give you any one or a combination of the following items in lieu of a raise:

- A nice bonus
- A top company award (large plaque)
- A vacation to a tropical location (like attending a week-long conference in Hawaii)
- Recognition in the company newspaper
- A nicer office
- Free dinner tickets
- Free tickets to the World Series or the Super Bowl game
- A promotion to a better position

- Personal laptop computer
- BlackBerry cell phone

You can name many other things here. The company can give you a whole host of things for the great job you did. So, *"ask and ye shall receive."*

You Must Have a Good Reason to Deserve a Raise

Asking for a raise is only warranted if an employee has good reasons for a raise, not just because he/she "feels deserving of a raise." For example, if the employee hasn't received a raise in two years and he/she has accomplished a lot of obviously good things for the company that everyone attributes to him/her, then and only then should he/she ask his/her supervisor for a raise.

> *Ask and ye shall receive.*

If You are Undeserving, Forget About Asking

If the employee hasn't done anything significant but come to work every day, work eight hours a day, and just do what was on the job description, he/she doesn't deserve a raise. In that case, I personally wouldn't ask for a raise. The employee would be laughed at, scorned, and/or chased out of his/her supervisor's office.

Accomplishments Deserving of a Raise

However, on the other hand, if the employee accomplished the following, he/she would have more of a case when asking for a raise:

- Brought in a large percentage of the company's revenue for the past two years
- Traveled widely for the company
- Sacrificed greatly for the company by performing many hours of free overtime work
- Garnered the company some valuable recognition for a major newsworthy accomplishment
- Saved the company a significant, measurable amount of money
- Performed major projects successfully for the company and received numerous letters of praise from customers
- Discovered, created, invented, innovated, and/or achieved major developments for the company during the past two years
- Landed major contracts or closed major deals

- Led a major proposal effort as proposal manager that won millions of dollars of new business
- Helped the company double in size largely because of the employee's efforts
- Solved a major problem the company has been struggling with for years

It Must Be Obvious to Everyone That You are Deserving

Do you get the picture? An employee must be "a mover and a shaker" in the company. He/she must "add value" to the company. He/she must "make a difference" in the company. He/she must be "a recognized go-getter" in the company. He/she must not only be well liked but one who "gets things done" in the company.

You Must Have Leverage

If an employee exemplifies all of these characteristics, he/she deserves a raise. Then, the employee has leverage, and when he/she asks for a raise, top management will listen and try to do something for him/her lest he/she voluntarily leaves the company for greener pastures.

Raises are Only for Those Who Build the Company

So, if one comes to work late every day, do very little, complains a lot, takes long breaks, and just passes the time away, he/she should not dream of asking for a raise. Raises are only for those who build the company, not for those who drain the company of cash by just being in spending jobs and collecting a paycheck.

Everyone Feels Deserving of a Raise All the Time

Unfortunately, everyone feels he/she deserves a raise all the time. This mindset is what makes life difficult for supervisors. However, if he/she does what is in the bulleted list above, then he/she can feel comfortable asking for a raise. If not, the employee should forget about it and be grateful he/she has a job!

Make a List of 10 Significant Accomplishments

In a two-year time-period, you should have accomplished great and wonderful things for the company. If you cannot make a list of 10 significant accomplishments (which are not in your job description) that moved the company forward, forget about asking for a raise. If you have accomplished at least 10 fantastic projects, you should have automatically received at least two raises by the time two years pass. If you have done great things and haven't yet received a raise, get out of there and work for a better company.

Most Employees Expect the World from the Company

However, what usually is the case is that most employees just do a passable job and they expect the world from the company. That will not fly! If your peers do not look up to you, you probably do not deserve a raise. If your peers do not automatically assume you should get a raise because of your performance and results, then you do not deserve one. When someone deserves a raise, it is obvious because of his/her great achievements, and everyone knows about them.

Get Off Your Fat Duff and Do Something

People who do very little but expect the world can find another job at another company. However, if they keep doing the same average job as they did in their previous company, they won't get a raise there either. Hence, the thing that they really need to do is to *get off their fat duffs* and discover something, create/invent something, innovate something, and/or bring in huge sums of revenue into the company. When they do that, then and only then do they deserve a raise.

What to Consider in Accepting or Declining a Promotion

I am currently in a situation where my company, Hollywood Video, offered me a promotion from a shift director to an assistant manager. This would require me to change locations to a store farther away, which just opened a couple of weeks ago. I've talked to every person who must approve the transfer request. I spoke with my store manager, my district manager, the store manager at the new store, and the district manager of the new store.

I have approval from everybody, but I do not believe they gave me a fair offer. The increase in pay, basically, covers my time and gas to travel to the new store. The job is, basically, the same but with more responsibility for the store. I do not believe I will take this opportunity. Is there anything else I should consider before accepting or declining the offer?

Considerations in Accepting or Declining an Offer

Everything we do depends on our values, motivation, and passion. From what you've already mentioned, you have made your decision to reject the promotion. Before accepting or declining this offer, you should consider the following items:

- *Impact on Your Future with the Company.* Will the decision to reject the promotion hurt you in the future with this company? If you're not going to make a career of this company, then it won't hurt you much. If you are making a career of the company, it may definitely hurt you. However, the degree of hurt is a function of the quality of your management.

- *Does it Help Your Resume or Not.* Will the promotion make my resume look better? Most definitely! It will create a bullet that packs a punch. Is that important to you?
- *Perception.* The promotion will definitely provide you with more experience, particularly for being responsible for the store. Even though you may feel that the job is basically the same as your current job, the perception of others, such as hiring managers, would be that the job was greater than your current job and contributed to your personal growth. That's just the perception generated, but *perception is everything.*

> *Perception is everything.*

I hope you wouldn't go into an interview and tell the interviewer that even thought the title of assistant manager sounds much better than shift director, it was basically the same job. Do you get my drift? A hiring manager would automatically assume that the assistant manager's position required much more work and responsibility than a shift director's position...unless you convince him otherwise of course.

Hence, perception of the better job title works automatically in your favor. That's why many people seek the title of manager. Managing the flow of cars is much more important than directing traffic because you would have a bunch of traffic directors reporting to you. Do you get that?

- *Negotiation.* You stated, "I do not believe they gave me a fair offer." Was this the result after you aggressively negotiated with them for the best offer? On the other hand, did you just accept what they offered you? If you didn't negotiate, shame on you. *Everything is negotiable.*

If you accepted this unfair offer, then that's all you're worth. So, if it is not a fair offer, counteroffer! You don't particularly want the promotion anyway. They want to promote you. Hence, you have all the leverage in the world to get a very good offer.

> *Everything is negotiable.*

You are in the driver's seat. You have nothing to lose but all to gain. So, why don't you use that leverage?

If you asked for the world and they withdrew the offer and promotion, so what! You didn't want the promotion in the first place. You lost nothing. But you put into their minds what you really believe you're worth. Do you understand what I am driving at here?

Negotiate the offer to the limit. Here is an opportunity for you to gain good experience negotiating to the hilt because you're not afraid of them withdrawing the promotion and offer. Do you get my drift? Ask and you shall receive.

In a way, I can see why you are considering rejecting the promotion. On your Jung Typology Test (JTT) or Myers-Briggs Type Indicator (MBTI), you are an ENFJ (Extroverted feeling with intuiting), and you are highest on "J" judging. Furthermore, on your Career Success Map Questionnaire (CSMQ), you scored high on "Getting Free" and "Getting Balance." The promotion satisfies neither of these two orientations. You're not the "Getting Ahead" or the "Getting High" type, both orientations of which you scored lowest.

Do What Makes You Happy

Whatever your decision, do what makes you happy. There is nothing worse than working a job that's pure drudgery to you. Since I believe your current passion is to become a financial investor or financial analyst, you should seek employment that allows you to work with money, capital, or purchasing power. These preparatory jobs could be a cashier, teller, accountant, or anything else that allows you to handle and/or deal with money. Then, leverage those preparatory financial jobs that will lead you to becoming a financial investor or financial analyst. That's the path you should take.

Mentor-Protégé Relationship Problem

Once I am in the corporate financial analysis industry of the investment banking area of finance, if I do not feel comfortable with my peers to establish a mentor-protégé relationship, how do you suggest I solve my problem?—Rigo Ortiz

Don't Work for Immoral, Illegal, and Unethical People

You will either be a protégé to a seasoned mentor or a mentor to a young, new recruit. If you do not feel comfortable with a particular young recruit, you can always get the relationship changed by talking to your management about it.

If you are a protégé to a seasoned mentor with whom you feel uncomfortable, again, you can request a change. Of course, doing that may be detrimental to your career particularly if your assigned mentor is an immoral individual. If that individual attempts to screw you, then it is best to find work somewhere else. You don't want to work with immoral, illegal, and unethical people…particularly with such executives in the company.

Establish an Informal Mentor-Protégé Relationship

If your company does not assign mentors, then you are on your own to find your own informal mentor. This is where your networking skills come into play. As you get to know all of the managers/executives in the company, you will gravitate to some and feel uncomfortable with others. The manager or executive with whom you can establish a personal, friendly relationship is the one with which you should establish an informal mentor-protégé relationship.

An Informal Relationship May Automatically Form

This relationship may form without the two of you even discussing or agreeing to it. If you go to lunch together periodically or socialize together, that would be good enough for you to ask for advice, guidance, and suggestions. When you receive good counsel from this individual, you establish a mentor-protégé relationship without the two of you even consciously agreeing to it.

Steve Schaefer—a Great Mentor

I have an informal protégé relationship set up with my informal mentor, Steve Schaefer. Steve has been a guest speaker in my Career Development class for a couple of semesters. Steve and I go to lunch together every three to four months. I have helped him on his resume, and he has served as a reference for me. We keep tabs by email and phone. It is a great relationship as we compare notes every time we get together for lunch.

Tarang Shah—a Great Protégé

I also have an informal mentor-protégé relationship established with Tarang Shah. Tarang has also been a guest speaker in my Career Development class for two past semesters. Tarang and I go to lunch together every three to four months. We have mutually served as each other's reference. We also keep tabs by email and phone. Like my mentor-protégé relationship with Steve Schaefer, Tarang and I have a great relationship as we compare notes every time we get together for lunch.

Establish Your Own Relationships

You can do likewise in establishing informal mentor-protégé relationships with your friends and business associates. This is another way to get ahead in the business and corporate world. Develop your network and establish those informal relationships.

Absence and Responsibility

I did some deep introspection about the comment that was made after I had said in class that students should not be absent willy-nilly from class. Then, a student retorted with the statement: "Then why were you absent from class on the second day of your new job to attend the evening off-site meeting social event?"

Minimized the Impact

This was the second day of my dream job, for goodness sake. I did not want to set a poor impression on everyone by being absent at this important evening social event. I knew that I needed to be absent for this class session weeks in advance, so this is what I did:

- Recruited Dave Blackledge to serve as a substitute teacher for me on that date
- Notified all students of my pending absence by announcing it in class as well as on the course website homepage
- Met with Dave Blackledge weeks in advance to prepare him for the class

Hence, I took responsibility for my absence by making sure that the impact on my students would be minimal.

No Responsibility Taken for Absences

In contrast, on average about a half-dozen students are absent from class each week. About two of them, on average, will responsibly notify me by email of their absence either before or shortly after the class.

However, the balance of the absent students don't bother to send me even an email to show me the courtesy by letting me know that they either will be absent or have been absent and why. Normally, these students do not even consider obtaining the materials or information that they had missed or will miss as a result of their absence.

Sign of What Has Happened in Our Society

The retort made above compared my absence stated above to those of students who show absolutely no responsibility whatsoever for their absences. This is just a sign of what has happened in our society, where we have lost all semblance of common sense and responsibility. To give you a better idea of what I mean, read the following piece from an anonymous source:

A Rather Remarkable Obituary

Today we mourn the passing of a beloved old friend, Mr. Common Sense. Mr. Sense had been with us for many years. No one knows for sure how old he was since his birth records were long ago lost in bureaucratic red tape.

He will be remembered as having cultivated such value lessons as knowing when to come in out of the rain, why the early bird gets the worm, and that life isn't always fair. Common Sense lived by simple, sound financial policies (i.e., don't spend more than you earn) and reliable parenting strategies (e.g., adults, not kids, are in charge).

His health began to deteriorate rapidly when well intentioned but overbearing regulations were set in place, e.g., reports of a six-year-old boy charged with sexual harassment for kissing a classmate; teens suspended from school for using mouthwash after lunch; and a teacher fired for reprimanding an unruly student, only worsened his condition.

Mr. Sense declined even further when schools were required to get parental consent to administer aspirin to a student; yet, he could not inform the parents when a student became pregnant and wanted to have an abortion.

Finally, Common Sense lost the will to live as the Ten Commandments became contraband; churches became businesses; and criminals received better treatment than their victims.

Common Sense finally gave up the ghost after a woman failed to realize that a steaming cup of coffee was hot, she spilled a bit in her lap, and the court awarded her a huge financial settlement.

Common Sense was preceded in death by his parents, Truth and Trust; his wife, Discretion; his daughter, Responsibility; and his son, Reason. He is survived by two stepbrothers—My Rights and Ima Whiner.

Not many attended his funeral because so few realized he was gone. If you still remember him, pass this on; if not, join the majority and do nothing.

Anonymous

8

Dealing with a Dysfunctional Workplace

As you look back over your career, do you see any patterns? Do you see a series of diffi-cult managers? Is your memory filled with challenging co-workers or uncomfortable environments? Are there several instances of expectations or dreams that weren't met?

If you see patterns or cycles, you're not alone. Sales professionals especially, can find themselves in a recurring nightmare of mismatched positions and lower-than-desired compensation.

What better time to set yourself on a happier course?[9]

Pat Schuler
Business Development Coach

Never work for a lousy, dysfunctional company. There are too many good to great companies out there. Why would anyone want to go to work for a terrible company? No person of substance would ever con-sider working for a dysfunctional company. Hence, seek the best companies and go to work for them.

Coping with a Bad Team or Bad Management

If you are satisfied with your job and your job responsibilities, how do you cope with being part of a bad team or management?

---

9.   Pat Schuler, "How do I step off the merry-go-round?," as quoted in the April 25, 2005, issue of *The Career News*, Vol. 5, Issue 16.

Working with Immature Workers

These days, you will have a few spoiled children in most work groups. They are adults, but they are just spoiled brats. All throughout their growing-up years, they gave their parents and teachers problems, and they will continually create problems for their boss and/or team leader.

The only way to deal with these overgrown children is to put them in their place calmly, firmly, and objectively...but fairly. They will whine, groan, moan, and complain. That's their tactic of getting their way. Ignore them. I had a few students like that in some of my classes.

Some Children Never Grow Up

These pathetic souls are crying out for attention. They attract attention by creating incidents or accidents. They may want to "push the envelope" to see how far they can go without someone lowering the boom on them. Some of these children never seem to grow up. It is pathetic to see them in their 40s, 50s, and 60 years of age. These people are a drag on society and on the company. These people populate loser companies. High performance corporate cultures would never tolerate this kind of behavior from their employees.

Get Rid of the Losers

I joined a company once and was asked to head a group of real losers. They continually fought each other like incorrigible juvenile delinquents. They were backbiters, backstabbers, and just a bunch of losers. I tried my best to get them to do the work at hand, but they refused to respond to directions. Finally, I took the problem to my boss, the vice president. We ultimately came to the conclusion that we needed to get rid of the entire group of losers and replace them with handpicked new hires.

Document the Performance of Losers

I did just that and built a high performance team. It became the most productive group in the company. So, as can be seen, sometimes drastic measures must be taken to discard the trash and bring in new blood that will be responsive to directions and produce volumes of high-quality work.

If you try to eliminate losers, you need to document everything you do with them. Keep a running record of every assignment you make. Document their progress (or lack of progress thereof), work quality, and attitude. Build up a factual, truthful, objective case against them.

Document Facts Unemotionally

You will need documented proof when you fire them, particularly if they make their grievance in a lawsuit against you and the company. If you have the facts unemotionally documented, you will be in a good position to defend yourself and the company in any litigation. *When you are prepared, you have no need to fear.*

> *When you are prepared, you have no need to fear.*

Dealing with an Unruly Co-worker

Just as with any other people-related problem, I would go directly to the culprit (whether it is your supervisor, co-worker, or anyone else) and present the problem to that person. Always attempt to work the problem out with the culprit. If the culprit is a reasonable person, you will be able to resolve the problem with him/her. On the other hand, if the culprit is unreasonable, insane, or a total wacko, you may not be able to resolve the problem. If you have made sufficient, reasonable attempts, tell the culprit that you will be taking the problem to management.

> *Never take a problem with a co-worker directly to management without first trying to work it out with him/her.*

Deal Directly with All Problems

Never take a problem with a co-worker directly to management without first trying to work it out with him/her. It is like going around your supervisor and directly to his boss. That approach is stupid, self-destructive, and counter-productive. Also, never ignore the problem. Deal with the problem directly with the people involved. *All problems should be dealt with in a professional manner.* There should be no yelling, screaming, cussing, or fighting. Deal with it on an adult-adult level, not on a parent-child level or a child-child level.

Communicating with an Inflexible Person

To communicate effectively with a co-worker who only sees things in black and white, you need to communicate in black and white. That's the only language an inflexible person understands. His/her mind is already made up. So, don't bother him/her with the facts. They only see things in binary, i.e., on or off, right or wrong, left or right, good or bad, and black or white. These people do not operate in the gray area. The gray area makes them nervous and insecure.

> *All problems should be dealt with in a professional manner.*

There are Certainties in Life

In certain areas of life, there is only black and white. For example, in morality, there is a right and wrong. In pregnancy, you are either pregnant or not. You cannot be half pregnant. You are either dead or alive. You cannot be half dead. One plus one equals two. That assertion is either true or false, correct or incorrect.

In Business, the "Gray Area" Usually Prevails

In other areas of life, such as in business, the "gray area" usually prevails. For example, upon listening to both sides of a disagreement between two co-workers, you may not be able to unequivocally establish who is right and who is wrong. In some cases, one may be right and the other wrong, but in other cases, the other may be right and the one may be wrong. So, who is right? Both may be right in some cases and both may be wrong in others. To come to an equitable decision, you need to compromise so that both parties would leave the discussion mutually satisfied. See, in business, everything is not in black and white. With human beings in the mix, this "gray area" situation prevails in most cases.

> *In other areas of life, such as in business, the "gray area" usually prevails.*

Strive for Synergy

Again, *in business, one plus one may not be equal to two. If we refer to "synergism," for example, one plus one may be equal to three, not two.* When something is "synergistic," the whole is greater than the mathematical sum of its individual parts. So, the work accomplished

> *In business, one plus one may not be equal to two. If we refer to "synergism," for example, one plus one may be equal to three, not two.*

when two co-workers work harmoniously, cooperatively, and in unison on a particular project, their total accomplishments may equal the total work of three co-workers instead of just the mathematical sum of the total work achieved by the two co-workers working separately and alone on the same project.

Work Harmoniously and Cooperatively Improves Productivity

This productivity improvement results because working harmoniously, cooperatively, and in unison together:

- Gets both co-workers down the learning curve quicker
- Improves and enhances communication
- Creates and optimizes ideas, through brainstorming, that are better when two heads work together
- Makes happier workers, and happy employees generally are more productive employees
- Assembles complex, difficult products quicker
- Moves heavy things quicker and easier with two people lifting than just one lifting alone
- Cheers on and motivates co-workers; hence, minimizes boredom
- Improves friendship and bonding and thus maximizes their productivity
- Optimizes work with each co-worker, through division of labor and handling things that each are better at doing because of education, talent, capability, and interest

Flexibility Improves Results

Hence, do you see that in business as well as in other areas of life, not everything is in black and white? Your co-worker who only sees things in black and white should learn that there are gray areas in life. She/he needs to be more flexible. Being flexible does not necessarily mean that she/he must compromise his/her principles, values, or integrity. We should never compromise these things. However, there are many other things that, if we were flexible, the typical results would be better and greater.

Handling Inappropriate Office Behavior

Management is always responsible for handling inappropriate behavior. However, as employees, when we see or are the target of inappropriate behavior, we are responsible for confronting the perpetrator and telling that person that he/she is doing something inappropriate and that he/she should stop it or he/she will get into trouble. If it is an egregious offense or the person continues to repeat that inappropriate behavior, we should then bring it to our supervisor's attention. After that, it is out of our hands.

> *Management is always responsible for handling inappropriate behavior.*

What Constitutes Inappropriate Office Behavior

Now, inappropriate office behavior may include any of the following:

- Sexual harassment
- Sexual intimacy (fornication) on the job between two employees
- Viewing pornographic materials on office computers
- Gambling
- Doing non-work related activities during work hours
- Soliciting
- Proselytizing
- Drinking alcoholic beverages
- Sleeping on the job
- Fighting in the workplace
- Discrimination
- Creating a hostile work environment
- Theft/pilferage/stealing
- Sabotaging other employees' work
- Doctoring records, timecards, and other data
- Vandalism

Receiving Backlash or Retaliation

Good supervision and/or management will take it from there to rectify or resolve the problem. If supervision/management ignores the perpetrator and inappropriate behavior, we have a final recourse, which is to contact the corporate ombudsman and confidentially bring it to that person's attention. Then, if nothing is done, we should forget about it. If you incessantly complain about it to everyone or bring it to the president's attention without the blessing of your supervisor, then you put yourself in jeopardy of receiving backlash or retaliation.

Don't Let Crooks Tarnish Your Good Reputation

If you work for a terrible company with immoral, unethical, or crooked management, nothing can be done. Simply get out of there as soon as possible or you will go down with the crooks and tarnish your reputation just by association. When top management is rotten to the core, if you attempt to do anything to correct a wrong, you will end up being the one who gets screwed. This is the situation where the messenger is killed. So, get out of there or end up being the fall guy!

Dealing with Theft

Yes, if you see workers stealing from the company, you should tell the manager about them. If you catch a lousy thief in action, you are not squealing on him or her when you tell the manager about it. You are just turning in a rotten crook! Any thief that swears to you that they will stop stealing is just adding lying to stealing. That person also cheats. For some reason, lying, cheating, and stealing seem to go together as a threesome. When someone does any one of those three infractions, chances are they are doing all three.

Bring Rats of Society to Justice

Hence, when you catch a liar, thief, or cheater, turn the sucker in to management. Those people only make things worse for everyone else who is trying to play the game fairly. Good companies have no need for these wretched people. They caused the Enron fiasco. They caused the WorldCom fiasco. They caused the Tyco fiasco. These rats of society need to be revealed and brought to justice.

No Need for Liars, Thieves, and Cheaters

They all started out small doing little nasty things and ended up screwing the entire corporation, the shareholders, the employees, the creditors, their customers, and themselves. In other words, they screw all stakeholders. Don't tolerate these rats. If you find any of these rodents within your workplace, turn them in to the proper authorities. We have no need for these liars, thieves, and cheaters in companies of integrity.

Dealing with an Unethical Boss

If you know for sure and have proof that your boss is doing business unethically, you should confront him with the evidence. If he takes it in the right way and works to correct the wrong, there is hope for this guy. However, if he gets mad at you and goes into a defensive/stonewalling mode, than that is a clue for you to get out of there at your earliest convenience. When the "you know what" (the thing that smells and exits the south end of a person or animal) hits the fan, he will attempt to blame you for it. Therefore, get out of there ASAP!

Many Rodents in Management Positions

There are many rodents like that in management positions in almost every company. You don't want to tarnish your good record and reputation by associating with such scumbags. Unfortunately, there are so many crooks, cheaters, and liars in business that sometimes you may wonder how you can compete and win by playing it straight. Have you ever played an honest game of Monopoly with everyone (except you) cheating? It is nearly impossible to win playing by the rules while everyone else ignores the rules and even makes up rules "on the fly."

What Can a Person of Integrity Do?

Here are the things you or any person of integrity can do in business:

- Perform business in an honest, upright manner and set a good example for others
- Correct all wrongs when you identify them or when someone brings them to your attention
- First, try to work it out with the culprit
- Next, bring it to upper management's attention if the culprit is incorrigible
- Then, if upper management ignores you, bring it to the attention of the corporate ombudsman
- Finally, if the company crooks attempt to get back at you, report it to authorities outside of the company, i.e., police, FBI, Defense Contract Audit Agency (DCAA), etc.
- Get out of there before you are tainted by the company you keep, i.e., if you cannot make the necessary corrections through proper channels
- Find and work for only outstanding companies that operate with integrity
- Start your own business and do everything with utmost integrity

Mischarging is a Fraudulent Activity

When I had worked at a major aerospace company, I had identified timecard mischarging (a fraudulent activity of charging proposal work to government contracts) that were being committed and brought it to my supervisor's attention. That must have stirred a ruckus. At first, nothing obvious happened. So, I asked him about it a week later. He then said that I did my job by bringing it to his attention so don't say or do anything else. In other words, keep my mouth shut and forget about it!

Kill the Messenger

Well, they then started to screw me. I lost my management position and was left to sit in the company library for over six weeks with nothing to do but read magazines before they gave me another position. Then, ultimately, when they had major downsizing layoffs, I was booted out the door with a whole bunch of others. Great guys!

Stonewalling as a Defense

I wrote to the corporate legal office, provided them with all the facts and details, and suggested that they should inform all employees to refrain from continuing this type of fraudulent activity. They just stonewalled me and said that everything was done in order and according to the law. It was sad. In my book, they were all just a bunch of crooks screwing the government. I was glad to be out of there.

How to Deal with a Meddling Boss' Wife

I have been working at my current office for about eight months now, and I have really enjoyed working there until recently. I have made great improvements in the office, and our numbers have doubled since I got there. However, now, they're starting to plateau.

I have been working with the doctor on things to improve in the office, but his wife (who does not work in the office or have any other affiliation with the office besides being the doctor's wife and an investor) is constantly bugging me. She calls a lot to find out what we can do and what is going wrong. I appreciate her concern, but it really gets aggravating. I know she has a lot of say in the office whether she is there or not.

How do I let my boss know that I could do my job better if his wife wasn't constantly bugging me? It just seems unprofessional that his wife calls me all the time, even if she is trying to help.

A Meddling Boss' Wife is Unprofessional

You are totally right! Your boss' wife is unprofessional by meddling in the office. If your boss has not already noticed that or have noticed it but has chosen not to do anything about it, then you are in "a real pickle."

On the Short End of the Rope

Whatever you do, do not talk to your boss about his meddling wife. If you did bring the problem to his attention and he talks to her about it, she will know that you had brought the problem to his attention. She will then be upset at you, and you will end up "on the short end of the rope."

Lose-Lose Situation

If your boss cannot maintain full control of his own office, then you can do nothing to either encourage or force him to keep his wife "out of your hair." Typically, we call this a Lose-Lose situation for you, i.e., no matter what you do, everyone will lose.

Work Only for Professional Organizations

Hence, I can see why you desire to quit after you have worked there for a year. It would be better for you to work for a more professional organization. Do it!

9

Quitting a Job

If statistics are true, more than half of U.S. employees dread dragging themselves out of bed each morning and making their way to work. And more than a few of these unhappy workers make a resolution each new year to improve their career by looking for a new job. Millions of these job seekers conduct their search while gainfully employed. The key is to keep the search discreet while maintaining job performance.[10]

Abridged: The Grand Rapids Press

Never quit a job before you have a better one securely in hand. Always stay in a job for at least a year before quitting and going on to something better. Always leave on good terms. Never burn your bridges behind you. If you do, it will always come back to bite you where it really hurts. *Always give a two-week notice when you quit.* Don't ever work for cheapskate companies.

> *Always give a two-week notice when you quit.*

Rejecting a Second Offer from Another Company

I just wanted to give you an update on my two job offers from Bank of America (BOA) and Washington Mutual (WaMu). I already accepted the WaMu offer, but I called and talked to the recruiter at BOA yesterday asking if what they offered was a set number. She said that the number they offered was what they start people off that do not have any banking experience.

She had to talk to the branch manager (where I would be working) to see if there is anything they could do. Today, I called back in the morning, and she said the branch

---

10. Abridged from *The Grand Rapids Press*, "Pursue a career move, keep current boss happy," as quoted in the April 25, 2005, issue of *The Career News*, Vol. 5, Issue 16.

manager said that there was no way to increase that number and to consider the benefits they offer such as medical, dental, vision, paid time-off, tuition reimbursement, and so on, and that it was a 20-hour part time position.

I'm not sure if WaMu offers tuition reimbursement. However, the difference in pay and what it will show on my resume is more important than tuition reimbursement would offer. Should I just call BOA and tell them that since I couldn't get a higher figure that I would have to decline? Or just send a rejection letter?

Always Keep Them Guessing

Do it either way, but do not tell BOA that you are rejecting their offer because they would not increase your pay as you desired. Tell them that you have decided to take the WaMu offer because they gave you more of what you wanted and leave it at that. Always keep them guessing. Do not ever reject them outright. Always make them know that their competitor pulled you away from their offer.

Never Burn Your Bridges

Never burn your bridges behind you. Always leave the door open to keep things available for future opportunities. Do it both in writing and in a phone call. Make sure you write your letter or email without any typographical, punctuation, spelling, or grammatical errors. Congratulations, and good luck!

> *Never burn your bridges behind you.*

How to Deal with Leaving a New Job Shortly After Joining the Company

If I accept a job and, after a couples weeks, I decide that this is not what I truly want to do with my life, should I find another job and still include this one in my resume? Leaving a job in such short time might reflect negatively on me, wouldn't it?—Jose Barajas

Due Diligence Required

Chancing a possible misfit is why it is important for you to take the time necessary to carefully analyze the hiring company before accepting their job offer. I try to drag out the offer, negotiation, and acceptance period as long as possible without turning off the hiring manager. You need the necessary time to perform due diligence on the company just as they check your references and conduct a background check on you.

Line Up another Job as Quickly as Possible

If the fit is untenable, it is best to get out of there as soon as you can find a more suitable job. If you can obtain another job within days, weeks, or no more than a month or two, you may not need to list that job on your resume as a past job that you would be required to explain the short tenure. If you were fortunate to have had two or three simultaneous offers, you could go back and talk to the people you had rejected to get them to reconsider you for hire.

Never Burn Bridges

This is why it is a good idea never to "burn your bridges behind you" but, instead, to reject companies in a very friendly, professional way. You never know when you may need to go back to them, and you will essentially be going back to them with "hat in hand." If you had burned your bridges, you could kiss off any possibility of getting one of those rejected companies to reconsider hiring you.

Never Hold a Full-time Job for Less Than a Year

If you drag out quitting beyond a month or two, then you should stay there for at least a year. An entry on your resume does not look good if you had worked there for less than a year (unless it was a summer job or consulting contract).

Easier to Find a Job When You Have a Job

You do not want to stay with a company for very long if your unhappiness will negatively affect your job performance. More than anything else, that substandard performance could be detrimental to your career. Additionally, if your unhappiness with the job negatively affects your health, then, get out of there before you end up in the hospital. At any rate, don't quit until you acquire another job, for *it is easier to find a job while you have a job*.

> *It is easier to find a job while you have a job.*

Prepare a Well-Written Letter of Resignation

When you do quit a company that you had joined only days or weeks earlier, prepare a well-written letter explaining that it was no fault of the company, but that you have just concluded that the fit was just not right. Explain to them that before it starts negatively affecting both your performance and health, you felt it was best to sever the relationship before it ends up being a lose/lose situation. Explain that you have been fortunate to accept another job that you feel is a better fit. Give your apologies and wish them luck in finding a suitable replacement. Again, do not burn any bridges as you depart from this company.

How to Quit a Job Properly

I was wondering what is the proper way of giving notice of leave to a company when you decide to quit. I work for an animal hospital and am thinking about pursuing some other job to gain experience in a different field. I just really do not know how to go about telling them that I am leaving. Is it proper to write a letter or just sit down one day with the office manager and let her know? Or is there really no proper way? Hope you can help me.

Let Them Down Easy in Your Letter

Yes, there is a proper way of quitting a job. Do both of your suggestions, i.e., write a letter and sit down with the office manager. Write a one-page letter that expresses:

- Your gratitude for working there
- How much you have benefited from working there
- Hope that you have made positive contributions to the animal hospital

Then, state that the time has come for you to experience a different field, and thank them for giving you the opportunity to work there. Give them a two-week notice of your termination in your letter. Make it a nice letter that lets them down easy.

Sit with the Office Manager

Take this letter into your office manager, say you are leaving the firm, and hand her/him the letter. Give her/him time to read the letter, answer any questions she/he may have, and repeat in words some of the things you wrote in the letter. Thank her/him for being a good office manager and bid your farewells.

Always Leave on a Friendly Basis

The office manager will either try to coax you to stay or will wish you the best. Either they will let you work the two weeks you have offered to stay before leaving or they will ask you to leave that day. Whatever the case may be, be very nice about leav-

> *Do not burn any bridges behind you.*

ing. *Do not burn any bridges behind you.* If you leave on a friendly basis, they may serve as a reference when you seek other jobs.

Recommend a Replacement

There are students aspiring to become veterinarians who would probably "give an arm and a leg" for the opportunity to take your job. If you are aware of such students, when you quit, you can recommend your replacement to the office manager. That would make them think very well of you.

What is the Best Way to Quit a Job without Burning Bridges?

I am planning to quit my current job as a store manager in December to start working on my master's degree in January. What is the best way to quit without burning any bridges, and when is it appropriate for me to give my upper management a notice? While I believe that a 30-day notice would be the best alternative for them to find a replacement for me, I am worried that they might say that if you don't want to work here anymore, why don't we just make today your last day? I've seen them do this to employees that put in two-week notices.—Roman Bogomolny

Always Be Cordial and Friendly

The best way to quit a job without burning any bridges is to do it in a friendly way. When you submit your resignation, let them know:

- How much you enjoyed working for them
- That you had learned a lot
- That you feel you have contributed to the growth of the company

Always be cordial and friendly. Express your regrets for leaving, but tell them that it is time for you to leave and move on to other opportunities for further personal growth.

Always Give a Two-week Notice

It is always appropriate and ethical to give a two-week notice. That is acceptable practice. Even if the company may let people go the same day that they submit their resignation, you should not duplicate that kind of unprofessional behavior. It is okay if they let you go the day you submit your resignation as long as they pay you for the two weeks period. Most of the companies that I have left paid me for the two weeks even if they asked me to leave that same day.

Don't Work for Cheapskate Companies

If the company you are leaving pulls such a stunt on you, be happy that you are leaving that company. With that kind of unethical behavior, it will some day catch up to them as more and more unhappy people leave that company. They will broadcast what a cheapskate company they left. With passing time, it all catches up with them (what goes around, comes around), and they will develop a reputation for pulling such stunts. If they do that to you, be glad you left.

Looking for Better Opportunities While at the Top

If you are at the top level of a company, should you continue to look for better opportunities elsewhere?—Ron Baclig

Always Look for Better Opportunities

Whether you are at the top level of a company or at the basement level of a company, you should always be on the lookout for better opportunities both inside the company and elsewhere. Always keep your feelers out, your eyes open, and your ears to the ground. Always keep an updated resume handy just in case someone asks you "out of the blue" if you are interested in a certain opportunity. *Always be willing to investigate any and all opportunities.* That's how you are going to get ahead in the corporate jungle.

> *Always keep an updated resume handy.*

Never Bluff Your Management

Now, when you say "top level of a company," you could either be at the vice president level or at the general manager/president/CEO level. Whenever you are offered a good position outside of the company, you will truly find out what your company thinks of you if they counter the offer or not.

> *Always be willing to investigate any and all opportunities.*

Never bring another offer to the attention of your supervisor or top management unless you are sure you would not mind leaving if they just abruptly said "goodbye" to you. In other words, never bluff them unless you don't mind being shown the door.

Investigate All Opportunities

If you are doing well in a company as vice president or higher, don't actively seek better offers elsewhere. Only if you fall out of favor with top management should you actively look for better offers elsewhere. However, even if you are well entrenched in your company as a high-level executive, investigate all opportunities if they come to you in an unsolicited manner. Never leave a good thing unless and until you have a very good offer from an outside company. They must give you everything you desire, or it will be a risky move.

Hold a P&L Position for at Least Four or Five Years

If you are at the top level of a company (i.e., general manager, president, and/or CEO), remain in that position for four or five years before ever thinking of jumping ship. It is smart to acquire good profit and loss (P&L) responsibility under your belt in these positions for at least four or five years. After that, you are then ready to take on a president or CEO position of a much larger company.

Opportunities Don't Knock Every Day

Remember, *opportunities don't come knocking on your door every day.* So, when an opportunity shows itself to you, do not "look a gift horse in the mouth." Investigate that opportunity and take advantage of it if it is an extremely good deal.

> *Opportunities don't come knocking on your door every day.*

Make sure you leave your company on good terms. This will allow you to work on joint projects together or return for a better position including a significant equity position in the future. Hence, never burn your bridges whenever you leave a company.

10

Education, Training, and Graduate School

According to the U.S. Census Bureau the difference in lifetime earnings between a high school diploma and bachelor's degree is a million dollars. Add on a master's degree and you can expect to get an additional half a million dollars in earnings. Those with professional degrees earn much more—about 4.4 million dollars during their working life.[11]

Staff Writer
The Career News

E ducation and training should be your lifelong endeavor. Never quit learning. Always stay ahead of your peers by reading constantly. Go to graduate school and get that master's degree and even that doctorate's degree. *Knowledge is power*. Therefore, always read, study, take classes, attend conferences, and advance your knowledge. That way, you will keep from becoming obsolete.

> *Knowledge is power.*

Reading is Important

On Average, Read 100 Pages Per Day

Remember, you should be reading on the average of 100 pages per day. If you don't do that, you won't be keeping up with your peers. In fact, you'll be falling

---

11. Staff Writer, "Education can be the key to your success," (Beverly Hills, California: *The Career News*, 2005), April 18, 2005, issue, Vol. 5, Issue 16.

behind and on your way to professional obsolescence. Don't become a dinosaur. Remember, they became extinct.

Read, Read, Read

You should always carry reading materials with you. Never sit idle anywhere (whether on the restroom throne, standing in line, riding a bus, sitting in a waiting room, or lounging/relaxing) without reading some-thing…anything. Those who will read during every spare minute of their day will learn more, make better use of their time, and advance their education. So, read, read, read!

> *You should always carry reading materials with you.*

Should I Take the Training and Run or Stay?

My question concerns taking an opportunity to receive quality training in a field that I might not be completely interested in. I began working with a loan officer in a reputable company as his assistant to learn more about the mortgage lending business. I was helping him with loans from the leads I generated, which was part of the training process.

I wasn't being paid as an employee yet, until I went through the out-of-state training program. I was told the training was paid, which to me meant airfare, room and board for the four days, and expenses. I find out three days before I'm suppose to leave that I am responsible for all expenses, which would total around $900. The training program is $5,000.

I'm thinking of taking the course to gain the knowledge and experience, but I'm not sure if I really want to work for that company, seeing as how they are already giving me the run around. So, should I take the training and work for the company to see if things change, which they probably won't, or take the training and work for someone else?

Listen to Your Conscience

That company may be "reputable," but if they continued with those kinds of antics, their reputation will fade away with time. Companies that cut corners, make you carry the burden, and give you "the run around" like that are basically cheapskate companies. I would not want to work for them. You already stated that you are "not sure if I really want to work for that company." That is your conscience speaking to you. Listen to it.

Life is Too Short to Work for Cheapskate Companies

Take the course, learn a lot from it, and then find a better company for which to work. *Life is too short to work for cheapskate companies.* There are many good companies out there. Find them and seek employment with them. Invest your time, energy, and money on companies who will carry out their part of the agreement and will look after you as you look after them.

> *Life is too short to work for cheapskate companies.*

Getting Company-Paid Training but Leaving Shortly Thereafter

I plan to leave the current office I am working at early next year. My boss has scheduled me to go to a seminar in January and February, and I probably won't be there past March. Should I tell him that I plan on leaving early next year to save him the expense of sending me to get further training since I'm not going to continue there, or should I take the opportunity for further education in my field? I mean, I will be there one to two months after the seminars, which is ample time to implement some positive changes in the office. What should I do?

It All Comes Out in the Wash

Take the training, get a better job, and don't look back. Most good companies provide company-paid training for their top employees. Everybody benefits from this training. People leave companies and people join companies. A company may lose the training they paid for an employee who leaves. However, on the other hand, that company benefits from employees they hire that had their training paid by other companies. It all "comes out in the wash." In other words, it equalizes out, and all companies benefit equally.

People Quit Lousy Companies

The only companies that actually lose educational/training investments in their employees are those lousy companies that have high attrition rates. People quit lousy companies. They quit companies that treat them like trash. Thus, their employees get what they can from their company and then quit at the earliest possible time after they receive the training.

Companies Should Treat Their Employees Well

If companies want to retain employees receiving company-paid training, then they should treat their employees well so they feel loyal to the company. A lousy company that loses good employees deserves exactly what it gets.

Don't Feel Guilty About Quitting

Learn all you can from the seminar, implement positive changes in the office, and then leave after you land a better job. Don't feel guilty about it. The company will get their money's worth when you implement positive changes in the office. Move forward, onward, and upward!

Graduate School or a Job after Graduation?

I am going to graduate this fall, and I do not know if I should continue with graduate school or, once I am finish with school, find a real job. I know that once you leave school, it is harder to come back. That is why I am thinking of entering graduate school right away.

Because of school, I have not been able to find a good job and concentrate in building my resume. How do you make the decision either to stay in school after receiving my BSBA degree or to find a real job for experience? Basically, what do you think is more important, education or experience, in order to get a good job?—Omar Garcia-Machado

Gain Good Experience Before Going to Graduate School

Once you graduate, you should work in a real job for at least three years before going full time to graduate school. Actually, if you have not yet been sending out your resume and garnering interviews, you are already behind the proverbial eight ball in capturing a real job that starts in January. Both education and experience are necessary to get a good job.

An Alternative is Night School

If it would be difficult for you to return to school after three years of full-time work, an alternative is to start right away and go to graduate school part time during the evenings and on weekends. This way, you may take anywhere from three to five years to complete your graduate degree. You will be working full time gaining good work experience and earning the money to fund your graduate degree. In this way, you continue your schooling uninterrupted while gaining good working experience.

Kill Two Birds with One Stone

I earned my BS in general business degree and MBA degree going to school part time taking evening classes. I took five years to complete my MBA degree. Hence, in my experience, I know it can be done. That would be my recommendation to you. Kill two birds with one stone, i.e., gain good working experience holding a full-time job and earning your master's degree by going to night school for three to five years.

Earning an Online Degree

Another alternative is to start an online master's degree program. You can study any time you have available in 24 hours a day and 7 days a week, i.e., 24/7. Several big-name, good universities offer master's degrees through distance learning (DL). I am planning to start an online doctorate program this fall with the University of Maryland University College (UMUC), University of Nebraska— Lincoln (UNL), or University of Phoenix (UoP). You can do likewise for your master's degree. There is more than one way to skin a cat!

When Should I Start an MBA Program?

After working in an industry for a while, when should you think about obtaining an MBA?—Anna Thompson

Rationale for Gaining Experience First

If you are going to graduate school for an MBA degree on a full-time basis, I suggest you work full time for three years first before you start full time on your MBA. There is a good reason for acquiring some "real world" experience before you start your graduate studies. Taking this approach allows you to:

- Discuss things more intelligently during class and group discussions
- Analyze and discuss your assigned case studies more effectively

Your Contributions and Understanding Will Be Better

When you have three years of actual, full-time experience working in a significant corporate environment, you contribute to discussions more effectively and gain a better understanding of textbook theories and assigned case studies.

Simultaneously Gaining Experience and Education

If you go to school on a part-time basis in night school and perhaps on Saturdays, then I would say you should sign up right away for graduate school particularly if it will take you three to five years to earn the MBA degree. It took me five years to earn my MBA degree from the University of La Verne in La Verne, California. As you work full time, you acquire "real world" experience over the three-to-five years to complete the MBA degree. Hence, you apply:

- To your job the classroom knowledge you learn while taking the courses over that longer time period
- The "real world" experience you acquire while working full time to the courses you take at a slower, part-time pace

Choice Between Full-time or Part-time Schooling

There you go. You need to choose whether you want to go full time or part time for the MBA degree. Whatever you decide, it will be the correct decision to go for an advanced degree. When you finish that degree, then you can consider going after the doctorate degree!

What is the Best Time and Method of Acquiring a Master's Degree?

Is it better to go to graduate school right after receiving my bachelor's degree, or is it better to wait and hope that the company I work for will pay for me and support me through graduate school? The reason I ask this question is because I have formulated my own pros and cons regarding each side, and professors I have had have given valid points for both arguments.

If this question isn't career related enough, then it could be asked slightly differently: Once I graduate and begin working, if I decide to go for my master's degree, would it be better for me to take a year off from work and take an intensive, one-year program, or would it be better for me to continue to work and take fewer classes over a longer period of time? Professors have also given me conflicting answers about this subject.

Work for Three Years First

The best way to do it is to work for three years before going into a full-time master's degree program. It is only wise to go straight into a master's program if you went to school late for a bachelor's degree. In other words, if you had worked for, say, 10 years and then went for your bachelor's degree. Then, it would be fine to go directly into a master's degree program.

Need for Meaningful Work Experience

If you went to college directly from high school to earn a bachelor's degree, then, it would be unwise to go directly into a master's degree program. Why? This is because you do not have any meaningful work experience to bring to the classroom and to make richer discussions. If you went that route, you would only be an erudite student. That means you only have book knowledge. You need some "real-world" corporate experience to make your master's program richer and better.

Your Answers Would Be More Intelligent and Meaningful

Does it not make sense that if you had real-world experience, it would be more beneficial to you as you do case studies in your master's program? You would bring your work experience into your analysis, and your answers would be more intelligent and meaningful. So, unless you have sufficient previous work experience, put off going for a master's degree for about three years.

Part Time is a Good Alternative

However, you have your free agency. You can do anything you so desire. If you want to start your master's program right after you receive your bachelor's degree, maybe you could make a compromise. Instead of going to school for your master's degree full time, you could go part time taking evening classes. This way, you would work full time acquir-

> *There is more than one way to skin a cat.*

ing good real-world work experience while taking a master's program that spans, say, over five years. In that way, you will become better with each passing year. You would simultaneously acquire good work experience as you learn advanced concepts in your master's program. *There is more than one way to skin a cat!*

There is a Good Reason for Experience

If the college or university that you attend for your MBA degree does not require any work or management experience, then you are free to go directly for your MBA. However, institutions of higher learning that require three years of either full-time work experience or management experience levy that on students for a reason.

One-way Transfer

If you are in a group of fellow students with this required experience, you are at a decided disadvantage because all you know is what you have read in management books. Those "real world" experienced students want to benefit from your experiences also. However, if you only have erudite book knowledge, then the "real world" knowledge transfer will be mainly one way. You will benefit much more than they will benefit. Can you see why most of the big-name business schools (B-schools) require at least three years of full-time work experience and even management experience?

The UCLA Executive Program in Management

Over two decades ago, as a general manager at HR Textron Inc., I was tapped to attend the 10-month evening course on "The Executive Program in Management" at the UCLA Graduate School of Management (GSM) back in February through December 1982. This course included 30 students who were practicing corporate general managers, vice presidents, presidents, and CEOs. It was a requirement that every participant possessed at least five years of management experience managing people, not things.

Management Neophytes Contribute Little

Can you imagine if we had students in there with no "real world" management experience? How could we have had meaningful, intelligent discussions with students without any management experience? We would feel robbed paying $5,000 in 1982 dollars for this high-level schooling if we had a bunch of management neophytes in the class. This is why top business graduate schools require at least three years of experience in all of their graduate students. Does that make sense?

First-tier B-Schools

If you apply to a first-tier school (e.g., Harvard, Stanford, MIT, University of Pennsylvania Wharton School, University of Chicago, et al), chances are you would need at least three years of solid work experience along with a very high GPA.

Second-tier State Universities

If you attended a second-tier state university (CSUSM, SDSU, UCSD, USD, et al), some may require a few years of experience and some may allow you to go directly from your undergraduate degree to graduate school.

Third-tier Schools

Even some third-tier schools (University of Phoenix, National University, Alliant International University, Excelsior College, et al) may require some work experience, but most of them will allow you to go directly from undergraduate to graduate school. Hence, it depends on what you want and what program you are qualified to enter.

Undergraduate Business Students Contribute Little

Have you noticed that we have little discussion and participation by undergraduate students in an undergraduate career development business class? Can you see these same students going directly to graduate school for, say, an MBA degree? With absolutely no "real-world," full-time experience in a large company, they would contribute very little when participating in case study discussions, solving business problems, participating in group discussions, and answering tough business questions.

Method to Their Madness

This is why top B-schools require at least three years of solid workforce experience before they would allow anyone into their MBA program. They must have some knowledge in their heads and experience "under their belt" so that they can carry on an intelligent discussion and write meaningful case study responses. So, there is method to their madness. If that does not make sense to anyone seeking a graduate degree, that proves he/she is unqualified to go directly from an undergraduate to a graduate degree program.

MBA, Apple Computer, or Farmers Insurance

Getting an MBA Directly or Later

As you know, I am unsure what I want to do when I am finished with school. I am seriously considering going for my MBA here at CSUSM. If all goes the way it has in the past, I will finish with a 3.5+ GPA, and I hope that is sufficient for our program. Do you think it is a good idea for me to pursue my MBA directly after I earn my B.S. degree?

I have heard from some people that I should go straight through, while others say I should get two to three years of work experience and then come back for it. I am not sure, but I honestly don't think I am going to want to come back in the middle of my passion/career pursuit. What do you recommend?

Yes, a 3.5+ GPA is sufficient to get you into many MBA programs including the one at CSUSM. I recommend you go to night and/or weekend school on a part-time basis to get your MBA. Read the responses to similar questions earlier in this chapter to get the full impact of my statement.

Possible Career with Apple Computer

Also, I have seriously been thinking about pursuing a career with Apple Computer as a business administrator or marketing manager. Do you think it would be beneficial for me to get a job at a retail store to get a foot in the door and some experience in the lower/hands-on part of the company? This all goes back to finding a job that I am passionate about, and besides music and God, I really love Apple computers, including the company itself.

Get Into Apple Computer in Any Way You Can

Apple Computer would be a great company in which to work. You should take preparatory jobs to prepare yourself to become a business administrator or marketing manager. If you can get into an Apple Computer retail store, do it. If you can get an entry-level job at Apple Computer in the lower/hands-on part of the company, do it.

Do Whatever It Takes

Whenever you can, network with Apple Computer employees. Attend job fairs where Apple is present and talk to those folks. Check out the Apple website. Apply for job openings they show on their website. Build up your resume to focus on getting into Apple.

Gain Computer Experience

If you cannot get a job working for Apple, then get similar jobs working for other computer companies that would provide you with relevant, transferable skills and experience for when you receive that Apple opportunity. Other computer companies that you could work for include Microsoft, IBM, Hewlett-Packard, Dell Computer, Compaq Computer, Motorola, Intel, Lucent Technologies, and Ingram Micro.

You Would Do Well as an Entrepreneur

Your CSMQ shows a "Getting Free" orientation. This indicates your desire for control over your own work processes, and you also want creative freedom. You desire minimal supervision, independence, and less structure. These are all reasons why your passions are in working with youth, playing music, leading the worship band, working with Apple computers, and selling. You would also do well as an entrepreneur.

A Slight Disconnect and Contradiction

What is interesting is that your JTT/MBTI four-letter code is ENTJ. You are an extrovert, which fits with your like of sales, music, and leading the worship band. However, there seems to be a slight disconnect between your "Getting Free" and your ENTJ. An ENTJ personality is in charge at home, and he expects a lot from spouse and kids. So, that is something you will need to be on guard against overdoing to maintain a happy home life. Here is where the real rub comes in: An ENTJ likes organization and structure and tends to make good executives and administrators. This appears to be somewhat contradictory of a "Getting Free" personality.

An Interesting Situation to Be In

Your "Getting Free" says you want less structure, yet your ENTJ says you like organization and structure, which are opposed to each other. So, you need to determine whether you desire less structure or more structure. This probably contributes to your being unsure of what you want to do when you are finished with school. I suggest you take some of the other free online tests on the Internet and nail down whether you are going to be more free, flexible, and independent or more organized, structured, and controlling. This is an interesting situation. Learn more about it.

Possible Career with Farmers Insurance

I also have another option. My Uncle lives in Kansas, and has a Farmers Insurance firm that he has successfully built up for many years. He earns a great living, and is getting ready to retire to pursue even more of his passions (more flying airplanes and traveling). Indirectly, he has basically offered me his business when I am finished with school. I would have to be trained and all of that, but essentially, his business could be mine within a few years.

Honestly, I don't feel called to Kansas, but I am wondering what you think of this opportunity. Sometimes I feel it would be a great opportunity for me to dive right into the business world, but I don't know if I am willing to move to Kansas. As I do not know much about the insurance industry, what would you recommend?

I know there are a lot of questions to answer here, but I would love to hear your insight and wanted to share these thoughts with you. Thank you very much for caring about us students so much to do this for us. I really appreciate it. I don't think I have ever had a professor that actually cared enough to coach/mentor students like this. Thank you!

Taking a Going Insurance Business Sounds Good

Your uncle's insurance business sounds like a good thing. He has an established clientele, which would make it easy for you to pick up and run with it. You could make a lot of money in one-fourth the time he did building his business from scratch over all those years.

Insurance Salesman Fits with "Getting Free" Orientation

An insurance salesman/agent fits in with your CSMQ orientation. As a "Getting Free" personality, you would have full control over your work processes as the owner of the firm. You would be on your own, so you would have minimal supervision. You would be an independent agent with less structure. So, an insurance salesman/agent fits in with your "Getting Free" orientation.

Extroverts are Good at Working with People

Being an ENTJ extrovert also fits in with being an insurance salesman/agent. You would be working with people and helping them achieve security against various risks. An ENTJ tends to make good executives and administrators. You would be president of your own firm and administering the insurance programs for all of your clients. So, ENTJ fits with being an insurance salesman/agent.

The Great Caution—Listen to Your Inner Self

Now, the great caution: If your inner self is telling you that you do not want to move to Kansas, then you had better listen to it. Pulling up roots and moving to the middle of nowhere Kansas will definitely be a cultural shock to you. Also, insurance is not the most exciting occupation in which to be involved. I took the tests and almost got involved in insurance sales once before. However, I listened to my inner self and got out of it before I "bit the bullet" and got entrenched in it. So, you need to really think hard about whether insurance can become a passion of yours or not. Also, think about whether you will be able to live out in the boonies.

For Some Reason, I Picked Oklahoma Over Kansas

When I was applying to attend college way back in the caveman days, I was accepted to both the University of Kansas in Lawrence, Kansas, and the University of Oklahoma in Norman, Oklahoma. For some strange reason, I picked the University of Oklahoma over the University of Kansas. If you like nothing but wheat fields, cow pastures, cattle, tornadoes, and only 2.7 million citizens, then Kansas beckons you.

Like Going from the Lips to the Armpits

I have traveled in 46 of our 50 states and have lived in about 10 different states, but nowhere else beats Northern San Diego County. Moving from San Diego County to Kansas is like going from the lips to the armpits. So, it is something for you to think deeply about before taking the dive. Once you leave San Diego County, it would be very difficult (mostly cost prohibitive) to return. So, choose correctly.

Difference between the MSBA and MBA

While many employers consider an MSBA and an MBA equivalent, a professor pointed out to me that the two degrees are different. From what I understand, an MSBA is for someone who did their undergraduate work in business administration; and an MBA is for someone who did their undergrad work in another discipline.

Also, after looking at San Diego State's FAQs (frequently asked questions) on their graduate program, I found that if I were to get my MBA, I would be repeating 19 units of curriculum. Why would anyone with a BSBA do this?

What is your opinion on receiving an MSBA vs. an MBA for someone with a BS in business administration? With regards to 'getting ahead of my peers,' wouldn't I have an advantage over someone who had an MBA if I were to get an MSBA (all other things being equal)?

Differences Between the Two Degrees

The MSBA and MBA degrees are different. The MSBA degree is a more technically oriented degree than an MBA, which is more general in nature. The MSBA degree concentrates on one of the areas such as general management, marketing, accounting and finance, human resources, organizational development (OD), international business, etc. The MBA is a terminal degree for most MBA graduates.

The PhD Degree

The MSBA degree is better if you later go for the PhD and further focus on one of the areas in business. However, many PhD-granting universities have programs where you can go from a BSBA degree directly to a PhD degree. A terminal degree, PhDs are usually for those who go into teaching, researching, consulting, presenting at conferences, and writing/publishing.

MBA Degree Good for Engineers

On the other hand, those who take the MBA program usually have degrees in other fields than business such as engineering, computer sciences, or liberal arts. For many people, the MBA is their terminal degree. For an engineer, the MBA is helpful particularly if the engineer decides to go into technical management instead of staying in the technical performance arena. The MBA helps the engineer to deal with people and the accompanying people problems. Whereas, prior to that point, his/her education helped him/her to deal mainly with numbers, equations, things such as laboratory equipment, and technical problems.

Repetition is Not a Bad Thing

The reason why you would repeat 19 units of curriculum is so that you get the material down pat, i.e., you understand it thoroughly. You must realize that you probably would use different textbooks (providing you with new and different subject matter), different instructors with different ideas, and different settings (classmates who come from all "walks of life" with varying work experience and knowledge level). Furthermore, repetition is not a bad thing. You remember things better and longer with repetition. If you feel you have the material down pat in these 19 units, then you should automatically get "A's" in all of these courses, which means you should get a 4.0 GPA on your master's degree program. Correct, right?

You Go Into Greater Depth with Each Subsequent Degree

Look at it this way. Should you go for a PhD in business administration, you will again be repeating most of these 19 units and the many other units you would have taken in your MSBA degree program. The whole idea is that you go into greater depth with each subsequent degree and that you understand the material thoroughly so that you can teach the subjects/topics with confidence and correctness. That's not all that bad is it?

Learn to Create New Knowledge

Further, as you dig deeper into the kernel of these subjects, you then will become knowledgeable enough, hopefully, to ask hard questions and to create new answers. My great dream is that you will be able to create new knowledge in these subject areas for your thesis in the MSBA program and your dissertation in your PhD program.

Become Creative and Innovative

The problem with many students these days is that they receive such superficial education that they are ill equipped to ask probing questions on one hand and to provide compelling answers on the other hand. All of this repetition and in-depth study of these subjects should help you to become so knowledgeable about those subjects/topics that you should become creative and innovative in your answers and your writings.

Come Up with Original Thoughts

Remember my question to all of you when I ask: *Have you come up with an original thought yet today?* Not many people do come up with original thoughts on a daily basis. When you learn a subject well enough through much repetition, you are then able to create new knowledge because you are unencumbered by clouded thinking and confusion as many students find themselves in when they cannot even differentiate between "marketing" and "sales," for example.

> *Have you come up with an original thought yet today?*

Lack of Understanding of Many Students

Students in our class cannot understand what a good bullet is! They cannot understand the concept of *"You are worth exactly what you accept."* After my constantly repeating it, they don't know that a resume and accompanying cover letter are sales/marketing documents, period! After constant repetition, I think (hope) they have gotten down the main purpose of a resume, which is to get them an interview. Sometimes, I wonder if that principle has yet been driven home in the minds and thoughts of some of our students.

> *You are worth exactly what you accept.*

People Need Repetition to Learn Things Well

Just by the wrong answers I get to the easy quiz questions that I give in class, I have come to the realization that there must be constant and unrelenting repetition for our students to learn well the principles being taught. So, don't feel bad about having to repeat 19 units. I know if I were to create a test of 100 questions from those 19 units of courses, nobody would be able to get 100 percent correct on all of the questions. That tells me that they need repetition of the things they had read, heard, and learned from the 19 units on the first go-around.

11

Self-Employment

What are you really good at? While we each have innate abilities to help us in this world, we need to know what they are and be aware of how we use them. Strengths are part of our passion. They are what we build upon and work with in entrepreneurship. It is important for us to connect to our passion through our strengths. Write down what you are really good at or what you believe that you would be good at, if you tried.[12]

Suzanne Mulvehill, MBA

E veryone who possesses the entrepreneurial spirit wants to start his or her own business some time in life. If you are that kind of person, don't put it off too long. Start that new business. You will gain a college education by learning about and doing the duties and responsibilities of the 35 or so hats that you will wear as a founding sole proprietor.

How Do I Start My Own Small Business?

Since my last posting, things have changed dramatically as far as a career path for me. Instead of the mortgage business, I am now going to partner up with developers in Florida, and through my own soon-to-be LLC, I will be marketing and selling these homes to investors in California.

This opportunity kind of fell into my lap. Even though I don't have much experience in starting and running my own business, I certainly don't want to pass on this opportunity. My question is this: Do you know where I can find information on starting, running, and maintaining an LLC?

---

12. Suzanne Mulvehill, "Entrepreneurs: What are you really good at?," excerpt from *Employee to Entrepreneur*. As quoted in the March 6, 2006, issue of *The Career News*, Vol. 6, Issue 10.

I am starting from scratch on this and will have to do everything from coming up with a name, logo, internal structure, and so on. Any websites or books you can recommend to me will be helpful.

Other Sources of Information

First, read chapter 11 on "Entrepreneurship" (14 pages) of my book titled *Career Quest for College Students*. Then, read chapter 27 on "Starting Your Own Business" (7 pages) of my book titled *Career Quest for College Graduates*.

Search Through "Ask Jeeves"

Next, go to "Ask Jeeves" at http://www.ask.com and plug in "starting a small business." Out will come hundreds, indeed thousands, of sources that you can read to get smart about starting your own business.

Visit the SBA

Next, go to the local Small Business Administration (SBA) office and pick up a lot of the free literature available on starting and running a small business. Also, you might consider taking a short course with them.

Talk to Entrepreneurs Like Todd Elder

Furthermore, talk to entrepreneurs who are successful in their small businesses. For example, talk to Todd Elder and many other successful entrepreneurs like him.

Checklist to Get Started

Now, you are ready to start your own empire. Here is a checklist of all of the things you might consider doing upon starting your small business:

- Create a unique business name
- Apply for a limited liability company (LLC) license with the Secretary of State of your state
- Apply for a Fictitious Name Statement with your local newspaper (go on the Internet to find the places you can apply)
- Get a location for your business (whether it is in your home or an office you can lease from someone)
- Obtain a mailing address and/or post office box for your business
- Create a logo and letterhead and get some letterhead and envelopes printed

- Create a business card and purchase a few hundred cards
- Create a mission statement
- Create a list of goals and objectives for each goal
- Prepare a documented SWOT analysis on your company's Strengths, Weaknesses, Opportunities, and Threats
- Put an announcement or press release in the paper about your new business
- Consider joining the local Chamber of Commerce
- Prepare a thorough, detailed business plan
- Get a business email address
- Start developing your network
- Open a business bank account and get checkbooks
- Establish the services of a good accountant, tax man, and attorney
- Join a couple of professional organizations in your career area
- Participate in these professional organizations
- Prepare a brochure on your company touting your qualifications, capabilities, and anything else going for you
- Establish an advertising program and obtain as much free advertising as you can
- Purchase and keep up an accounting journal of all of your income and expenses
- Keep accurate records (for tax purposes) and save all receipts of your purchases
- Develop your products and/or services
- Purchase/lease office equipment such as computers, calculators, copying machine, fax machine, telephones, stamp machine, file cabinets, desk, chairs, working table, etc.
- Get dependable, hard working, honest key personnel
- Establish your business website
- Purchase business liability insurance and errors and omissions (E&O) insurance
- Sign up a firm to do your paychecks, accounting, and taxes (Paychex and ADP are good examples)
- Prepare company policies and procedures

Just the Beginning

This is just the beginning. There are many, many more tasks to perform in starting your business and keeping it going. You will be wearing 35 hats until you can achieve sufficient cash flowing so that you will be able to hire employees. You will not be able to do justice until you can hire at least five or six full-time employees. To do everything by yourself is too taxing. You need to delegate much of the legwork and menial labor to direct reporting employees.

You Need Capital to Succeed Quickly

Also, if you are going to run your business on a shoestring, it will be very tough to get things going quickly. If you can start out with $100,000 in your bank account (a million dollars would be even better), it will make things easier for you. If not, you will struggle for years until your business can get some traction. Good luck in starting your new business!

What if I Want to Be an Entrepreneur Who Wants to Keep My Business Small?

I have read the chapter on entrepreneurship and find the suggestions and comments very informative; however, the chapter seems to specifically speak to the entrepreneur who wants to make a big business fast.

I am considering starting a business on the side, something that is seasonal and can be done at home and on the Internet. Specifically, I am considering starting a gift basket business on the side and partnering with a friend who owns a shipping store. The idea is to combine our collective business knowledge and use her store and my creative design capabilities to make gift baskets for special occasions and holidays.

While our business plan has only been conceptualized, I am wondering if you have any advice for the entrepreneur who wants to keep things small?

The Business will Stay Small Automatically

You don't ever need to worry about your business "getting out of hand" and growing large, particularly if your desire is to keep it small. No entrepreneur grows a large business if she/he didn't have a goal to make it a large business. Most new businesses (about 90 percent) go "belly up" within five years anyway. I don't know of anyone that had a business grow automatically without any effort. Hence, if you want your business to stay small, don't worry about it. It will stay small and won't ever grow rapidly out of your control. Just don't put too much effort into it.

Mom-and-Pop Shop Mentality

The reason why most (nearly all) home businesses remain small and not grow rapidly is that owners do not spend the necessary time, effort, and money on the business to make such growth happen. If you have the "mom-and-pop-shop" business mentality, your business will remain small.

Growth Mentality Needed to Grow Big

You must have a growth mentality for a small business to grow into a large business. In other words, you must think big. If you don't think big, your small business will never grow big.

Why Most Business Don't Grow Fast

Even then, however, most entrepreneurs cannot and do not make their businesses grow fast. This is the case because of one or a combination of the following reasons:

- They have no attractive, in-demand products or/or services that meet unmet needs
- They do not have the necessary start-up funds
- They do not have the necessary talent in the key functional areas (i.e., management, marketing/sales, engineering/R&D, manufacturing/QA, finance, and human resources)
- They lack a good business plan
- They do not have a good, identified market niche in which to operate
- They do not possess a competitive edge

Most Small Businesses Verge on the Brink of Survival

Most small businesses do not have these things going for them. That is why they remain small and usually verge on the brink of survival. So, don't worry about your business growing fast and large without your desiring it to do so. Your wish will happen automatically. Personally, I would "go for the gold." In that way, you would at least have a better probability of survival.

12

Potpourri of Topics

1. *A combination of incongruous things: "In the minds of many, the real and imagined causes for Russia's defeats quickly mingled into a potpourri of terrible fears" (W. Bruce Lincoln).*

2. *A miscellaneous anthology or collection: a potpourri of short stories and humorous verse.*[13]

Dictionary Definition and Pronunciation
Yahoo! Education

This chapter is a *potpourri* of thoughts I had that didn't fit easily into any of the previous 11 chapters. It covers topics such as taking courses, whom to marry, the color red, taking tests, and the givers and takers of the world. These are provided as food for thought.

Do Not Worry About Passing a Career Development Course

Whenever you take any course (whether career development or otherwise), you should be more concerned about learning things that you can apply on your job and your life than in just getting a good grade. Many college graduates enter the work world with good GPAs, but they cannot do much to help their companies make money and grow. They don't know how to be creative and innovative. They wait to be told what to do instead of using their initiative and creating their own work.

---

13. From The American Heritage® Dictionary of the English Language, Fourth Edition. Copyright © 2000 by Houghton Mifflin Company. Published by the Houghton Mifflin Company. Quoted in the Dictionary of Definition and Pronunciation, Yahoo! Education website, Copyright ©2006, extracted on 5/29/06 from http://education.yahoo.com/reference/dictionary/entry/potpourri.

Do the Assignments and Learn a Lot

So, you shouldn't worry about passing the course. Just do the assignments, and good grades will automatically come. What I am really concerned about is this: *"Have you learned anything from this course, or have you just been to class in body only?"* It is better to receive a "C" and learn a lot than to receive an "A" and be ignorant of everything that I have attempted to teach.

The Important Take Away Ideas

Here are the things I want you to take away from the Career Development course and this book:

1. *Integrity is the Most Important Thing.* Always remember that your personal integrity is your most important asset. Always tell the truth and never lie, cheat, and/or steal.

2. *Your Attitude Determines Your Altitude.* Your attitude is the most important tool for your success. *Your attitude determines your altitude.* Is your glass half full or half empty? Always look at it as being half full, not half empty.

3. *Expect the Best and Be the Best.* Expect the best and get it. Be the best of the best. Always strive to be world class.

4. *What Really Counts is Doing.* It's not what you know that counts. It's not who you know that counts. It is what you do that really counts.

5. *Three Types of People.* Regarding accomplishing things, there are three types of people in this world. Those who:
   (a) Watch things happen,
   (b) Make things happen, and
   (c) Always seem to wonder, "What happened!"
   Always be the second one, i.e., make things happen.

6. *Bullets That Pack a Punch.* Perform superbly on your future jobs so that you will be able to easily write resume bullets that pack a punch, hook, grab, and wow hiring managers. Remember, your bullets should be of your performance, achievements, accomplishments, and results. Your bullets should be quantified, measurable, truthful, reasonable, time-phased, and meaningful. Your bullets should have a feature and a benefit. That's it. Forget about bullets that are just job descriptions, duties, and responsibilities.

7. *Pursue Your Passion.* Seek and work at only what you are passionate about. *Isn't it great to get paid for having fun?*

8. *Compete and Be the Best.* Always compete and strive to be the best in the world at whatever you do. If you do that, the world will come running to you, and you won't need to go to the world to get the goodies.
9. *You are Worth What You Accept.* You are worth only what you accept…no more! So, ask and ye shall receive.
10. *Everything is Negotiable.* Everything is negotiable. So, negotiate! If you won't negotiate, be happy with what you get.
11. *Perseverance and Endurance.* Never give up; never give in.
12. *Original Thoughts.* Have you come up with an original thought yet today? If you haven't, start now to be creative, innovative, and original. Write it down!
13. *Three Interview Questions.* Never leave an interview not knowing whether you are going to receive an offer or not. Ask the three most important questions at the end of the interview. Question 1 is on the company goals. Question 2 is the company strategy to achieve those goals. And question 3 on whether you meet their requirements for the job.

Apply What You Have Learned

That's it, folks! If you learn these things and you receive a "C" in the course, you will have accomplished more than all of those who received "A's" but didn't learn a thing. Then, of course, the most important thing is to apply in your life what you have learned.

Most Important Decision: Whom to Marry

The Right Spouse Will Be a Real Asset

One of the most important factors about successful career development is whom you marry. Select well and you won't have as many problems as you would have if you selected the wrong person. The right spouse will be a strong supporter, facilitator, and helper…in other words, a real asset. The wrong spouse will be a real drag, drain, and frustration to you…in other words, a real setback. I was fortunate to have found the right forever person (my wife, Karen) for me.

Top 10 Areas of Preference in a Mate

One of the keys to healthy mate selection is deciding what type of person you want in your life. In order to determine who will mesh with you to create a brilliant, loving, and long-term relationship, you have to spend some time examining the various human dimensions. Dr. Neil Clark Warren has highlighted the following 10 dimensions for consideration:

- Intelligence
- Personality
- Appearance
- Ambition
- Chemistry
- Spirituality
- Character
- Creativity
- Parenting
- Authenticity

Take these 10 traits and rank them in order of importance to you. It will be difficult to meet someone who is perfect for you in every single category. If you've ranked them, you will already know which are essential to you and on which you are willing to compromise.[14]

Real Success is True Happiness

Remember, real success is true happiness…not fame, fortune, and power. Also, remember, success in marriage is something you must work at, for it does not happen automatically. Like everything else at which you succeed, you must work at it. Good luck, friends!

Red is Generally Good!

I have another suggestion on the use of red ink to correct papers. You should only use red ink when something is wrong or needs to be changed. Don't write "good job" or "great" in red ink. Red is generally bad. You didn't really discuss that in your findings. It's just a thought.

Good Things About the Color Red

Regarding correcting papers with red ink, I take issue with the statement that "Red is generally bad." I say, "Red is generally good." The only significance of the

---

14. "What You Really Want in a Mate," from the eHarmony.com Newsletter, ©2000–2006, eHarmony.com, Inc., http://www.eharmony.com/.

color red is that, next to black, red is easier to see on a white page, which is a good quality. For example, here are some good things about the color red:

- When something is red hot, that's good!
- Some people like red cars because red means hot. The red car is also the easiest to spot speeding by law enforcement officers. That's proven out by studies.
- Roses are red. Women like red roses.
- A Valentine heart is red. Red stands for love.
- Some people love red wine. To them, it's good.
- Red in the saying, "Red rover, red rover, send so-and-so over" is neutral…not a bad thing.
- In politics, there are blue states and red states. That doesn't have any negative connotation to it. The blue states are primarily liberal states, and the red states are primarily conservative states.
- Redskins aren't bad. It stands for our Native Americans as well as a nickname for a professional football team (the Washington Redskins).
- Christmas is represented by red, green, and white. Nothing negative there. Santa Claus wears a red suit, and the children love him.
- "Red Skies of Montana" was a great movie about forest fires in Montana…fire being red. Fire is good. It provides heat that warm us. It cooks our food.
- Red hot chili peppers are great. I love them.
- During high school senior proms, boys wear a red carnation boutonnière, the girls wear red corsages.
- Blood is red. It is used in transfusions. If we didn't have red blood for transfusions, many people would die. Hence, red blood is good.
- Someone said red represents death. Not so! Black represents death. The Grim Reaper, who represents death, wears black. Witches wear black clothing and hats. Widows wear black clothes to funerals. The hearse is black. The hearse carries the dead.
- The Red planet, Mars, is so called, but does it mean Mars represents something bad or negative? No!
- The American flag's colors are red, white, and blue. Is red bad in our flag? No!
- Is it bad or negative that some people have red hair? Redheads are beautiful.
- A red blush or flush is not necessarily bad.

- Red space on a roulette wheel, red checker pieces as well as the red and black checkerboard, and red clothing are not necessarily bad. Some people desire red clothing, particularly some women.
- I don't have a single red cent represents a copper penny. That's not really bad. Pennies are worthless anymore anyway.
- I can go on and on and on.

Where Red Represents Something Negative

The only cases I can think about where red represents something negative include the following:

- In financial circles, when a business is operating in the red, that's not good. If it is operating in the black, then that's good.
- We used Red to represent Communism for many years. To us it is bad; however, to the Russians and Red Chinese, red is good. Who are we to establish the good and bad connotation of colors used throughout the world? Red is good and bad depending on your perspective.
- I know that people use the color red to represent the devil. But that's just a label we put on it.
- Red capsules, a barbiturate or drug, may have a negative connotation to them.
- Red eye or red eyes may not necessarily be good.
- Red with anger may not be very good.

Red Maximizes Visibility

Thus, the statement "Red is generally bad" is not a true statement. Red is generally good! Whether the red ink is use does not mean it represents errors on a page. We use red only because it maximizes the visibility of the comments on a page whether the comments correct an error or makes a positive statement. Additionally, corrections are good!

Red is Good!

Hence, people who complain against red ink start from a faulty premise that created a study. The study showed results that support my assertion, which indicates that red does not represent anything bad in correcting papers. It just represents a color that is easier to see and read than any other color except black. Since the words on a white page are black, then the next best color to use to highlight errors, make suggested corrections, and praise good writing instances is RED! That's it! Red is good!

Taking Tests/Quizzes

Test Taking Guidelines

The distribution for all tests is usually normal (normal distribution; bell curve) with the curve usually skewed to the right. Students should always write their names and date on the test or quiz sheet. That is the first duty you do before you start reading the questions. Always, always place your name and date on the test/quiz (or any other piece of paper for that matter) first before doing anything else. The next thing is to follow the directions. Next, read each question carefully. Finally, go with your first instinct.

Know the Material Cold By Doing Your Homework

Some students will know the material cold. Hence, they will mark the correct answers without any hesitation. I usually write the word "Genius!" next to their circled overall score. This is what I want students to do.

Be Decisive and Confident of Your Answers

Don't be hesitant on your answer decisions. Decide and mark your choice of the answer. Don't look back. Don't hesitate. Don't rationalize yourself out of the correct answer.

Don't Copy Someone Else's Answers

Especially, don't look at your neighbors' answers and change yours by copying what he/she has marked. If you copy someone else's answers, it indicates you lack integrity…much less confidence in your own selections.

Read and Highlight Important Points

If you read the assigned chapters, review the PowerPoint presentations, listen in class, and read all of the materials posted on the course website, you will do well on the tests/quizzes. When you read the textbook materials, you should highlight the key, important points.

Use Sticky-back Notes for Easy Retrieval

Mark the pages with small, yellow sticky back paper to flag out the important pages. Since I always have open book tests/quizzes, students should quickly be able to find their marked pages and verify their answers. Why some students do not do that is far beyond my comprehension.

Two Kinds of People in the World

In relationships, there are two kinds of people in the world:

1. Those who generally lean towards being givers
2. Those who generally lean towards being takers

Givers are Better Networking Nodes Than Takers

I appreciate all those in my classes who are "givers" instead of just takers. Those students who "give" are excellent networking nodes. I want to network with only those who are "givers."

Positive, Constructive Testimonials from Givers

I appreciate all those in our class who are givers. They have written some great testimonials included in Appendix D. These students have given positive, constructive testimonials of this course. These are the kind of students who I want to keep tabs of throughout their careers. They take from me, yes, but they also graciously give to me. They are good networking nodes, and they understand that principle well.

What Goes Around Comes Around

What you don't want to ever be is a giver of only negativism and destructive comments about everyone and anyone…including your instructor. Because if you do that throughout your career, I promise you that you will be a receiver of negativism and destructive comments in return. "Whatever goes around comes around." Dish out crap, and you will receive crap all of your life. Don't be that way. Dish out good things, and good things will come your way.

The Principle of Reciprocity

My best students have learned this principle well. I will bend over backwards to help any student (or anyone else for that matter) if they exercise being a good networking node, which is *You scratch my back, and I'll scratch yours.* There is equity in that kind of *quid pro quo* arrangement. Some people never learn that principle of reciprocity throughout their miserable lives. That's why they will lead miserable lives and will be unsuccessful at whatever career they pursue.

Dish Out Warm Fuzzies

In this world, you cannot do everything by yourself. You need others to help you, just as others need your support and help to be successful. Remember that principle for the rest of your life. If you don't dish out two warm fuzzies for every one warm fuzzy you receive, you will always be left wanting. Learn and exercise that principle and you will receive many good things throughout your life.

Honesty is the Best Policy

Avoid Falsification

I had a past student who falsified the evaluation of his mock interview. I didn't punish him, but I felt very sorry for him that he had to write up a false evaluation. He must have felt guilty about it (which was a good sign) because he came to me and confessed. Friends, it's not worth it to lie, cheat, and steal. By doing that, you hurt no one but yourself.

Voluntarily Confess When Required

I had another student that came to me and told me that she really didn't have a perfect attendance record as I had shown on my score sheet. She admitted that she had missed a class and, therefore, didn't deserve the 25 extra-credit points. Because she came to me on her own volition to tell me the truth, I felt good about her and told her that I was going to give her the 25 points anyway because of her honesty and integrity.

APPENDIX A

Examples of Personal Brand Statements (PBSs)

Personal brand statements (PBSs) uniquely identify or brand individuals. It sets you apart from everyone else. The following PBSs were created by my Fall 2005 MGMT 445 Career Development class students:

Armacost, Stacy—Bright, organized, confident professional with diverse experience offering excellent interpersonal skills actively pursuing challenges head-on

Baclig, Ron—One who enjoys all the hobbies of life with a passion and determination for success

Barajas, Jose—Ambitious, hard working leader dedicated at achieving superior results while helping others achieve their own

Belmonte, Leah—Wonderfully easy to befriend, honest, reliable, vivacious, confident lady inspired by the ability to succeed

Bogomolny, Roman—I am an experienced manager with great management and marketing skills ready to help your company increase sales

Brockhaus, Andrew—Ambitious learner, leader, and implementer with the ability to build, develop, and maintain meaningful relationships

Daniels, Johnny—Johnny is an honest, loyal, free-thinking individual who is motivated to reach a successful balance

Daniels, Ty—Innovative hard working computer guru and student with excellent interpersonal skills who's anxious to graduate

DeNobrega, Greg—Providing outstanding sales and customer service with honesty and integrity

Espinoza, Angelina—Dedicated and trustworthy business oriented woman who can succeed at any job presented to her

Garcia, Catalina—A team player, problem solver, ready to undertake the most challenging task with a smile

Garcia-Machado, Omar—Ambitious man who has managed to overcome challenges and believes everything is possible with hard work

Garrow, Darren—Darren Garrow, striving to maintain a balanced life and stay loyal to those most important

Griego, Katherine—An intelligent, highly organized, reliable, honest, trustworthy, hardworking woman who strives to succeed in life

Hall, Jennifer—A dynamic, innovative problem solver you can depend on to precisely execute projects to completion

Heatherman, Michelle—Goal-oriented, organized, ambitious, trustworthy, multi-tasking, team-player who strives to create quality and efficient results

Mak, Melinda—A student who is motivated by the success created by challenging myself through hard work

Martinez, Matthew—A Trustworthy and Efficient Competitor, an Innovator of logical and detailed solutions to complex problems

McCamish, Alison—A hard-working, ambitious, trustworthy, organized, multi-tasking, team-player who strives to create quality and efficient results

Morris, Lindsey—A hard-working, intelligent woman who will go above and beyond to get any job done

Murphy, Heather—A hobby pursuing, goal-oriented planner dedicated to obtaining a balanced work life and personal life

Ortiz, Rigo—An honorable, courageous, optimistic hard charger ready to accomplish the mission no matter the obstacle

O'Sullivan, Lauren—Dynamic and creative young woman, continuously working hard to succeed in order to ultimately achieve

Seguine, Nicole—Aspiring to be an influential leader with values who motivates others to accomplish their dreams

Smith, Angela—Determined Confident Leader in makeup artistry world who creates powerful, inspiring faces and attitudes

Smith, Dustin—Creator of innovative ideas with a passion to succeed while continuing to develop winning habits

Thompson, Anna—Encourage others to reach greatness and strive to be the best person they can be

Tijerina, Summer—Unwavering, vital and ambitious, perceptive, always directed, detailed and definite, confident, determined, encouraged and hopeful

Tobin, Michael—Using innovative ideas and perspectives to accomplish tasks through the utilization of collaborative, creative thinking

Tran, Steven—A hard working, dependable, and organized individual who can manage time and responsibilities

Upper, Lauren—Enthusiastic personality with passion and motivation about giving the best customer service possible to everyone

Viveros, Eva—Hard working, ambitious, reliable team player who excels in life and strives for the best

Appendix B

Occupational Analysis Report (OAR)

The occupational analysis report (OAR) is a written report that a job seeker prepares on a particular occupation of interest and discusses his or her fit for that particular occupation. Rigo Ortiz prepared the following excellent example of an OAR.

Becoming a Finance Master—By Rigo Ortiz

Why I Consider the Financial Analyst Occupation

I have considered the financial analyst occupation because it serves as a means to an end. In other words, the occupation is not an end in itself, but it serves as a vehicle for me to ascend into executive management positions. With experience gained from employment and a few more years of graduate work, I will be prepared to handle the duties and responsibilities of an executive management position.

I plan to obtain two graduate degrees—Master of Business Administration and a Master of Science in Management with a concentration in Finance—to keep my employment options open. However, I am undecided as to which graduate schools to attend.

Demands

After interviewing Tarang Shah,[15] an investment associate at Softbank Capital, and researching the 2004–2005 edition of the *Occupational Outlook Handbook* (OOH), I found some interesting facts of the occupation. A financial analyst assesses the economic performance of companies and industries for firms and institutions with money to invest.[16] Also, financial analysts go by other names

---

15. Shah, Tarang. Investment Associate, Softbank Capital. Interviewed him on 10/13/05.
16. *Occupational Outlook Handbook*, www.bls.gov.

such as securities analyst, investment analyst, or investment associate. Further, according to the OOH, banks, insurance companies, mutual funds, pension funds, securities firms, and investment banking firms supply employment locations to financial analysts.

Long work days is the first demand to explain. According to Mr. Shah, the investment banking industry is notorious for demanding an extreme amount of working hours per day—more than 14.[17] Also, the information provided by Mr. Shah concurs with the OOH, which states that financial analysts may face long hours.

Next, financial analysts must travel quite frequently. For instance, the analysts visit prospective companies for investment, or the analysts go on outings to meet with the clients and other high-level representatives of firms. When I interviewed Mr. Shah, he informed me that he was in San Francisco visiting investment bankers two days before I had interviewed him. Further, he said that his position does not require him to travel out of the country. His focus is on domestic private firms that might be interested in going public. In accordance with the prior demand, the OOH also mentions that travel comes with the job.

A third demand of the occupation is deadlines. According to Mr. Shah, he must quickly research volumes of financial statements and other information in an abbreviated time span. With this speed needed to meet the deadline, Mr. Shah mentioned that the right judgment helps him to decide to call or not call a potential company a second time. He calls a company a second time only because he is interested in investing in that company. However, time is of the essence, so good judgment is required to select which company to contact again. As with the above demands, the OOH noted that the pressure of deadlines comes with the job.

In addition, mathematical, computer, analytical, and problem-solving skills are required of candidates striving to become financial analysts. I would say that Mr. Shah fulfills this requirement. For example, his undergraduate work is in technology and engineering, disciplines that require the skills noted in the opening sentence of this paragraph. Then, he graduated from Thunderbird University with a Masters in International Management to give him more exposure to analytical problem-solving theories. Even more, he now holds a level two Chartered Financial Analyst (CFA) designation that gives him a technical and credible foundation in finance. Agreeing with the prior demands noted above, the OOH also states that financial analysts should possess mathematical, computer, analytical, and problem-solving abilities.

---

17.   Shah, Tarang. Investment Associate, Softbank Capital.

Finally, financial analysts require communication skills in speaking, writing, reading, and listening. After I spoke with Mr. Shah, I discovered that he makes numerous phone calls to representatives of potential companies for investment. Also, he has to go through the financials of the company for deciding to invest or not invest. After he gathers the required information, he presents that information to the partners of his venture capitalist firm. Additionally, the OOH mentioned the importance of oral and written communication abilities to financial analysts.

Incentives

The rewards of the financial analyst occupation are quite interesting. For example, according to Mr. Shah, some financial analysts have the luxury of setting their own hours. The life of a workaholic is not appealing to him. So, he enjoys the role of an investment analyst, and he also appreciates the benefit of living a balanced lifestyle. On the other hand, the OOH mentioned that some financial analysts will be burdened with the laboring long hours each day.

One other important incentive of the occupation is to be at the forefront of the market. This insight comes from Mr. Shah. Since he is in one of the 5,000 positions of investment associates of venture capitalist firms in the world, he possesses a unique opportunity to choose what products he sells on the open market. He acquires about $250 million from investors and performs the research with his team—at minimum, the team includes a lawyer and a technology savvy person—on prospective private companies to see which one will go public.

My Fit

According to the Myers-Briggs Type Indicator, I enjoy the ENFJ—extrovert, intuitive, feeling, and judging—type indicator. My minimal extrovertedness fulfills the demand of communicating with other people both verbally and in writing. Since I like to project the possibilities for the future through looking for the big picture of the macro environment, I can handle the analysis of the relationships between firms and the economy required by the financial analyst profession.

On the other hand, my feeling type, instead of judgment type, does not match the thorough analysis conducted by financial analysts although I do strive to improve that weakness. However, because I have the judgment type indicator to close in on a goal when I do not have all the data, I still have an opportunity to succeed as a financial analyst, for they need to make quick decisions.

I had earlier mentioned my aspirations of achieving an executive level position, and I know that finance is a path to my career destination. I feel and know my above noted academic achievements provide me with opportunities to realize my career goals. Consequently, I am glad that a career is not an end in itself.

I must find a career that will satisfy my values—family, time, health, peace, love, success, and wealth. In the final analysis, the incentives of the financial analyst position might not fit the big picture of my career expectations, yet I will live the financial analyst experience as part of paying my dues. After all, great things come to the man or woman who does good work with integrity.

APPENDIX C

Situation-Action-Result (SAR) Stories

T he situation-action-result (SAR) story is a written piece that a job seeker prepares on a particular job situation and discusses how he or she handled and resolved that situation. Several students prepared the following excellent examples of SAR stories.

Supervising Nightmare!—By Stacy Armacost

Situation

Being a director at my job has its advantages and disadvantages. I think the problem lies primarily with my age due to the fact that the employees I oversee are all quite older than me. Of course, I know myself and my personality, and I know that sometimes I can come across maybe too demanding. However, I only expect from my staff what my boss expects from me.

My position on this type of work ethic situation is that, no matter if you are a line staff, manager, or CEO of the company, ALL should be giving 110 percent. To me, that is not too much to ask. The employees who work only for a paycheck are the ones you must watch closely. They will stab you in the back for sure. It has been a challenge to gain the respect of the employees and to be effective and efficient in the production of work.

Action

My first step was to take a supervisory training course and gain the skills and abilities to communicate effectively without sounding too in charge or egotistical. I was able to grasp the concept of requesting work to be done in a manner that did not offend the employee, which is at times not very easy to do.

In addition to the training course, my boss, who is the executive director of the company, mentored me. She is amazing and is one of the smartest women I have ever met. She has taught me so much when it comes to being a manager. She really had to get it across to me that not everyone is like me. I think that is what was the hardest for me to realize, i.e., that everyone works at a different pace and registers information in different formats.

Result

I found that there are three types of employees: Type A, B, and C. Type A's are the ones you definitely want to hang onto who make you shine and go above and beyond the call of duty. Type B's are doing a good job but not going above and beyond to prove themselves. Type C's are the ones you want out of your company NOW. They are the poison that brings down the morale of other employees and creates a hostile work environment.

It has been over a year now, and it seems as though I have managed to relate on the same page as the staff as well as bite my tongue on many occasions. Tremendous progress has been made in this situation, and I feel that the staff think of me not as some young girl who just wants to be "in charge" but, instead, as some young woman who is trying her hardest to do a good job and to provide excellent service to the elderly residents.

I think that they also realize that I also have a genuine interest in their well-being and truly care for our team's accomplishments. Of course, the road will never end, but I am willing to take it for all its worth.

Operation: Respect—By Andrew Brockhaus

Situation

One weekend, my boss, a co-worker, and I went to Sacramento for a conference. When we arrived at a hotel room, something came up between my boss and my co-worker. Referring to a past occurrence, my boss began to yell and use profanity with my co-worker. It was humiliating for her and very uncomfortable for everybody within the room.

Action

While my boss was yelling and using those vulgar words, I intervened and, in a calm voice, told him to calm down, and that we didn't need to talk like that to each other. He looked at me with a weird look, but I politely continued to tell him that he needs to calm down and that he should stop talking like that.

Result

My boss did, in fact, stop yelling and swearing, and the situation eased down. He left to go into the conference, and my co-worker was left crying, feeling humiliated, and ready to get on the next plane home. I stayed and helped her to feel better and encouraged her to stay. She did stay, and it turned out to be good for them to be able to deal with this situation.

I was not okay with how my boss had treated my co-worker, and I talked to him about how we need to treat each other with dignity and respect. He was receptive and ended by apologizing to both of us for his actions.

Disgruntled Customer—By Johnny Daniels

Situation

Working as a valet, I dealt with a high volume of customers on a daily basis. Not every customer is a happy one. During track season at the Del Mar Fairgrounds, business is at its most chaotic time. I was working at The Beach House in Cardiff during a Friday night right after the races ended. People were trying to get in to watch the sun set and spend their winnings.

Usually, we can move cars quickly to maintain the flow of people. A customer who had been drinking felt he could drive through the exit and skip everyone in line. Since he drove a nice car, he thought he deserved special attention and wanted to park his car close to the entrance. After explaining to him how he skipped the row of cars waiting for 10 minutes, he became hostile.

Action

During those times, when the lot is at full capacity and it is physically impossible to park another car, we have to shuttle cars to a separate location. This guy wasn't standing for that. I've dealt with these types of situations and people before, so I knew what had to be done. I calmed the guy down by being calm myself and explained to him how things work, and that his car would be taken care of respectfully.

I pointed out the fact that he pulled a risky maneuver by crossing the median on Coast Highway to drive into the exit of the restaurant where he proceeded to lash out in a drunken rage. There are many cops patrolling the area looking for this type of behavior. I told him that as well, and he understood. After talking for a while and smoothing things over, he thanked me and gave me $20 to keep his car close, which we did.

Result

My patience and problem solving abilities benefited here greatly. As the guy left the restaurant a little more sober, he thanked me again and gave me another $20 for "putting up with him" and taking care of his vehicle. Since that day, he has become a regular customer, and we've become friends.

Everything in Life is Possible—By Omar Garcia-Machado

Situation

One of my biggest challenges in life has been coming to a different country and not knowing almost everything about the culture. I was raised in Tijuana, Mexico, but my family decided that it was important for me to have the choice of coming to the USA and continuing my education.

When the moment arrived of my coming to a different country, I was really scared about it. However, I then realized that it would be something really brainless to stay in Mexico. I have learned that opportunities seldom come twice in life and that was and has been the biggest opportunity of my life.

Action

I decided to come and, at the beginning, it was really difficult since my language barrier was the biggest obstacle for me. I knew it was really easy just to stay in Mexico. However, I wanted to show everyone that I was capable of working on my weaknesses and reaching my goals.

For the first year, I took a bunch of English classes and read a lot as well. After slightly more than four years, I have learned to speak, write, and argue in English, which is basically at the same level than someone that has been here for 20 years.

Result

Everything is possible in life, but it just depends on you to make it happen. It takes a lot of determination to do something that, when you start, seems so far away. I was really ambitious throughout my career as a student and still am, which I know is going to take me really far in my career inspirations. I was capable of managing many obstacles and finding a way around them.

Assisting Students with Math Problems—By Melinda Mak

Situation

Kumon Math and Reading Center is an after-school program for students in kindergarten through high school. It is a program to assist students with math problems and to teach new math problems.

I came across one individual who was so fed up with himself for not understanding how to do a page of math problems. He wanted to give up and not continue with the program any longer. He was constantly asking his parents to take him out of the program. His parents told him that he needed to stay with the program to help him succeed in the future.

Action

I sat down daily with this student. I worked through each math problem with him. When he did not understand a step that I was doing, I told him to stop me, and I would explain to him again what I was doing. I continually worked with him and told him not to be fearful of asking questions. I constantly assured him that no question is a stupid question, and that I would offer him any assistance needed.

After I showed him step by step on doing a math problem, I would have him do similar problems on his own. After completing each problem, he showed me his results. If a step in his problem was incorrect, I would carefully explain to him what he did wrong while constantly reassuring him that it was okay to make mistakes because he is still learning.

Result

This student became confident in himself. I reassured him that if he did not understand a problem that it would require more concentration and hard work to understand and solve it. His parents were very pleased to see that their son did not give up. They thanked me for being so patient and understanding with him.

His parents approached my boss and told her what a great job I did with their son. They were very pleased at how much their son has learned. He learned that he is capable of doing anything and never to give up if a task becomes more difficult. He learned that the more difficult the problem, the harder he must work to solve it.

Kids Day America Team—By Lindsey Morris

Situation

I had a huge event coming up at my work called Kids Day America, and we were all feeling very overwhelmed. The communication between the three of us planning the event was not good either, thereby leaving us all stressed with no clear idea of our individual tasks.

Action

Feeling extremely overwhelmed, I took charge as leader of the event and delegated the tasks among the three of us. I also established a weekly meeting to discuss our progress in the previous week, brainstormed our plans for the following week, and acquired help that we needed on our individual tasks for the event.

Result

After two-and-a-half months of excruciating work, our event went off without a hitch, which gained all of us great recognition from our boss. We were also given the next large event to plan since we did such a great job!

The Black Hole—By Lindsey Morris

Situation

I once worked in a small office with four of us employees crammed into a small two-desk work area. We were very limited on space, so our supplies, files, and event boxes all ended up in the only place we had room left, which was the storage closet also known as "The Black Hole." This closet was large, but we could never find anything we needed because it was so cluttered.

Action

On a weekend when our boss was out of town attending a seminar, my fellow employee and I took an entire day to reorganize "The Black Hole." We weeded through what was and was not needed, put on labels, and organized all shelves. We even moved an extra desk into the closet to give us more work space.

Result

When our boss came back the following week, she could not believe her eyes. Not only did it make finding items more efficient, but it also gave us more space to work! It really helped improve our flow in the office, and our boss asked us to do her closet next!

Killing with Kindness—By Angela Smith

Situation

While working at the San Diego Credit Union, I have had my share of run-ins with different co-worker personality types. I have always been known as someone who could just let things people do roll off my back and not take it personally. One such incident occurred when I was promoted to my current position five years ago.

A fellow employee warned me about this woman at my new branch who would most likely give me a hard time. Apparently, she was notorious for doing this to new employees. So, when I started working at my new branch, I was sure to be extra nice to this woman. However, it did not matter, and I inevitably made her mad for some reason that I cannot even remember to this day since it was so insignificant. However, I do remember how I handled her.

Action

When this co-worker confronted me very rudely, I was initially shocked and did not know exactly how to respond. After returning to my desk, I thought about how I could handle this without having to run to management. So I decided to go to my fellow co-worker and ask her what I did to upset her and why it had upset her so much.

I explained that I was sorry for anything I may have done to offend her, and she just stared at me with no response. I apologized again and told her I hoped we could get past this incident and move on.

I left her desk, and she then confronted me again in the hallway telling me that I should not have confronted her at her desk because the manager might have heard us. I told her I wasn't trying to get her in trouble. I was just trying to work things out.

As the months went by, I continued to kill her with kindness. I would give her a compliment here or there and tried to be her friend. She resisted quite a bit until one day when she was feeling very ill. She does not drive, so she could not drive herself home. I offered to drive her home immediately and worked it out with the manager.

Result

As a result of this, my co-worker finally came around and treated me like an equal. She could finally see that I did not have any motives other than trying to be her friend and co-worker. We were finally able to get along very well from that day forward. We have even become very close co-workers who help each other out as much as possible. She has even made sacrifices on her days off to help me out when I have been in a jam.

Getting along with everyone has always been my "cup of tea," and I have always been successful at it. She was the hardest egg that I have ever had to crack, but it was worth all the effort. I think killing someone with kindness is always a good approach to getting along with someone that isn't always the easiest to get along with.

Fixing an Outage Problem—By Angela Smith

Situation

While working at the San Diego County Credit Union for the last seven years, I have definitely learned the ins and outs of branch operations. I would probably be an assistant manager by now if I was not going to school full time due to the fact that any management position is full time, and I only work 30 hours a week.

Due to my experience, I am often called on by management to help with problems that arise. One such situation came up recently when a new manager was closing and balancing the branch. One of the tellers was out of balance in his cash and checks. They looked and looked for the outage and could not find it.

Action

Upon becoming aware of the situation, I immediately went over to help the teller so that the manager could continue balancing the rest of the branch. We found the causes of his outage and fixed them.

One of the outages was difficult to fix because the teller gave a member credit for a $208 check that did not exist. The worst part was that he had cashed the check and had already given the money to the member.

I then voided the transaction and re-posted it correctly. This correction caused the teller's cash drawer to be out by $208. I then called the member and left him a message to let him know that the teller had accidentally given him too much money.

I called the member right away so that he would not spend the money. I left the member my phone number and asked him to come into the branch the next day or to call me. I helped the teller balance the rest of his cash drawer, and we left for the night.

Result

While I was working the next day, the member came in to return the $208 that he had received from the teller. He said that he did not even realize that the teller had given him too much money. He was glad that we had called him promptly to rectify the situation. He returned the money to the teller, and the teller was able to fix his cash outage from the previous day.

This was a great result for two reasons. First, if the teller had not found the outage, he would have been written up and had a negative statement in his file. Second, the teller and manager were very thankful to me and said that they could not have fixed the problem so promptly and effortlessly without my help.

Reservation for 30, Please!—By Summer Tijerina

Situation

I am currently a server at Chili's Restaurant. Chili's is a casual family dining restaurant. In practice, we normally do not take reservations. However, we do appreciate calls-ahead, which are when large groups give the restaurant a fore-warning that they will be eating at Chili's.

On a particular evening, I was one of two closing servers. The night was slow, and many servers had already been sent home. Thirty minutes before closing, the hostess received a call that a party of 30 people would be arriving in 10 minutes. Apparently, a local play had just ended, and a father of one of the actors had invited the other cast members with their parents to celebrate their child's birth-day after the play had ended. The father gave an estimate of 30 guests; however, 75 people arrived!

Action

At Chili's Restaurant, any table larger than 12 people requires that two servers attend to it. We only had two servers available for all 75 guests. The manager began to get frustrated as more and more guests arrived. Children ran around everywhere and were sitting at tables with no adults.

Both my co-server and manager were overwhelmed. My manager was visibly frustrated, and I could tell that he was beginning to affect the father who brought in all of the guests.

At this point, I took the initiative to organize the entire group. I stood on top of a chair and whistled loudly. I then introduced myself and the other server and explained the process of how we would take orders so that everyone would enjoy dinner.

Since there were so many kids with no identified parents in sight, I announced that orders would only be taken from the parents and that the parents would deliver the food to their child.

Result

The result is that two servers were able to feed 75 guests in a timely manner. This was no easy task. The father pulled me aside and thanked me for handling their large, unexpected group. He then stated that I should be the manager as I took the necessary steps to calm the crowd and get everyone organized.

My manager also complimented me on organizing the group so that we were better able to serve the guests. The approach I took in addressing the large group was also complimented. While I was loud and direct, I used a sense of humor to make my points. The resultant atmosphere was less stressful as the guests were informed of the process to be used.

Long Lines…Oh-Oh, Seizure Attack!—By Eva Viveros

Situation

While working in the Admissions Department at Palomar College, this particular day was like no other day. Not only was it very hot, but the air conditioning was malfunctioning, and it was during the energy crisis. We had long lines of students wanting to apply, register, or get on the wait list for classes.

I was working at the front counter when I called to assist the next student in line. The student came to my counter and handed me her application and registration papers to add classes. As I processed her application, as we normally do, all of a sudden, she was no longer in front of me, but she was on the ground.

Students in line were yelling and screaming, "She's having a seizure!" This was the beginning of something altogether new to me. I did not know the first thing about how to handle such a situation, but I quickly learned.

Action

When the student was no longer in front of me, I quickly went to the other side of the counter. I held the student down so she would not kick or hit other students and/or injure herself. Another student assisted me as well, and we tried to keep the student down and, at the same time, tried to calm other surrounding students to give us room for air.

I had a co-worker call our Health Services Department, and the supervisor (who was at lunch) later came to assist. The nurse came shortly after the call, and my assistance was no longer needed. I went back to the counter and saw the ambulance take the student away for extra care.

I finished processing the student's application, got her registered in her classes (it was a good thing all her classes were available), and called her to let her know that her registration was completed. I also followed up the call with an e-mail to let her know that she was registered and to tell her that if she needed anything else to give me a call.

Result

The incident was unfortunate, but our department learned from this ordeal. Not only did our department have a meeting about how to handle similar situations in the future, but I was acknowledged and praised by the vice president and director of Student Services for taking the proper action and steps to get the student assisted in a timely manner.

I was acknowledged for staying calm and acting quickly yet effectively. A few days later, the student and her mother came to see me and handed me a bouquet of flowers for taking care of her and for completing her registration process. She was pleased to find that she got enrolled in all of her desired classes. Additionally, her mother liked the fact that I had called and left the e-mail message.

Bad Cake Day—By Eva Viveros

Situation

My father owned a bakery. From time to time, I would go into the shop to help him out. I would not call this a job. If anything, I would go to eat sweets.

On a Saturday morning, which was my father's busiest day for cake pick-up orders or other special orders, a young lady came to pick up her cake. She mentioned that it was her daughter's first birthday party, and they were excited. I gave her the cake, and she was on her way.

About 30 minutes later, she came back and was crying stating that she got rear ended, and the cake was thrown to the floor of the car. She had the box with her, but the cake was ruined. She asked if we had another cake that we could sell her, but we did not have any. She was saddened and did not want to settle for just a grocery store cake.

The cake my father had made was a "*tres leches*" (included three different types of milk). The lady was sobbing, so I called my father. He was out of town and told me to take care of the situation as best as I could.

Action

I spoke to the lady and told her to come back in about three hours. She understood that we needed time as this was a "rush" situation. She said that she would come back in three hours.

Since we had a baker working that morning, I asked him to prepare another cake. He did not know how to decorate the cake, which then became another problem. My father was the one who decorated the cakes. Luckily for me, I had watched him do it and had picked up on a few designs.

When the cake was ready, I gave it a shot and, thank goodness, all came out okay. Minus a few decorations that should have been air brushed (I did not give it a try), I decorated the cake with anything we had on hand and made it look as if it was one of my own.

I was rather impressed with my work. After all, having no training, I only saw and observed my father decorate cakes. I called the lady, and she came to pick up the cake. She was running late but informed me that she would come.

Result

What had appeared to have been a bad morning for the young lady turned out to be a great day. She loved the cake and could not thank me enough for what I had done for her. She insisted on paying for the cake, but because her day started off so badly, I decided not to charge her. She was very gracious to both the baker and me for taking the time to make the cake on such short notice.

My father returned, and I explained to him what I did. It turned out that she was one of his best customers who would refer more customers to the shop for their bakery needs. She helped my father get more clientele. He was happy with the decisions I had made that day, so he gave me $40. To me, that was enough as I was still in high school.

The young lady later spoke with my father and gave many thanks for my understanding and was amazed at what a great job I had done. This was just one happy customer that brought more customers to the shop.

APPENDIX D

Testimonials

Testimonials indicate what people think about something. Positive testimonials give an idea of the effectiveness that a course or teacher has had on students. The following testimonials are from students in the fall 2005 MGMT 445 Career Development class:

- I know there are many questions to answer here, but I would love to hear your insight and wanted to share these thoughts with you. Thank you very much for caring about us students so much to do this for us. I really appreciate it. I don't think I have ever had a professor that actually cared enough to coach/mentor students like this. Thank you!
- I wish that all of the professors at CSUSM had the same positive attitude as you. I believe that your class should be a graduation requirement. I truly enjoy your class and believe that it will be very beneficial for me in the future.
- It's very nice to see someone so passionate about his students. I think you are a great "manager" and am doing my best to keep you impressed!
- You are a great professor and leave a great impression on all your students.
- I have told many friends of mine about how great your class is, and they would like to take it next semester.
- Thank you for the inspiring email. I think it's great that you are actively involved in your student's grades. It is a shame that you won't be here next semester; CSUSM needs more professors like you!
- This is one of the best courses that I have ever taken. If you will be teaching classes at a graduate level or anywhere else, I will gladly take another course from you.
- I am happy to have taken your class since I am now armed to obtain an employment opportunity that will serve as the means to an end to realize my dreams. Thanks for being a great, positive teacher. I have enjoyed the experience of participating in your course and meeting you.

- This was an excellent class. I enjoyed it very much! Thank you very much, Professor Uda.
- I enjoy navigating through your website a lot now. It is quite interesting once you get familiar with it. Thanks for putting so much time and effort into preparing it for our class.
- Since this is your last semester teaching this course, I think you would be the perfect business professional with tons of expertise in this field. You should definitely come back and speak with other students who will be taking this class in the future. Your input to the students would greatly help them. Glad I took this class!
- It's too bad that you won't be here next semester to teach this class. People are really going to miss out.
- This course can help every business student. There is a lot of information that you get out of this course that you won't get on your own. I think each student should learn how to do a resume that has bullets that pack a punch and put together a career portfolio. This was a very good course.
- My resume writing skills improved giving me greater confidence when trying to get an interview. This class is great, and I would recommend this course to every business student.
- It's been a pleasure to be in this class with such wonderful students, who I was able to network and build relationships with as well. Thank you, Professor Uda, for all the hard work you put into this class. I know you are really bogged down with your new job and trying to juggle many things at once, but you are very good at it, and I respect you for being such a positive, optimistic professor, who sees the best in all of us.
- After taking this class, I am constantly looking for better ways of improving my skills to gain more knowledge in different areas and build my resume. Whether it is taking additional classes related to my current job or looking for new jobs that will allow me to learn new skills, I think that this class has helped me realize that a variety of skills and continued learning is only going to add to my success.
- This course has really taught me how to market myself to get the career of my dreams.
- Hey, Professor Uda, I just wanted to say thanks for the e-mail. It meant a lot to me. After all, I learned a lot from you. Your class really made an impact on my career. Thanks again.
- Thank you so much for taking the time to give me a thought out response to my virtual coaching (VC) question. You have definitely given me insight, and I will try to take things as they come as I strive to achieve.

- I truly have been honored to have had taken your class. I will definitely take with me more information than you can imagine. I cannot put in words just how much your class has given me more to think about. I am forever grateful for all I have learned and will take with me in my career. Thank you so much for your words of thought, wisdom, and for giving us examples of great real life experiences.
- This class should definitely be required for every business major senior. From the first class that I attended, I looked at you as a friend rather than a professor. This might explain why I have perfect attendance in this class.
- I wanted to also thank you for everything that you have taught me in this course. My cover letter and resume look 10 times better than before. I went into this course with little confidence in my resume and cover letter. I definitely see the value in having "bullets that pack a punch" and how they can definitely differentiate my resume from those of other candidates. Thanks for everything. I enjoyed your class.
- Thanks for your help. By the way, your last lecture to the class was my final lecture as an undergraduate. It also happened to be the most honest and most motivating one I have listened to. It will stand out in my memory of my college experience. Thanks, again, Mr. Uda.
- Thank you, professor Uda. I am happy that I have taken your class this semester. The articles and the virtual questions and answers have been very beneficial to me. The only sad part is that you won't be teaching at CSUSM next semester. As you taught us in class, "go where the opportunity is and never look back." In this case, I wish you the best in your new career.
- I just wanted to say good luck with your new job. I hope you continue to keep in contact with some of us, and I'll let you know how things are going. I enjoyed taking your class and I am sorry to hear that you will no longer be here. You were a great teacher, and I hope you enjoy your new dream job. Thanks for everything.
- Professor Uda has done such an amazing job at providing the students with all the necessary tools and resources, not to mention detailed instructions regarding every assignment in the class and for the personal career portfolio (PCP).
- You kick A$$, Mr. Uda. You are inspiring, motivating, and very helpful. Thanks, Mr. Uda.
- Good luck with you new job!! I will see you around, and I really enjoyed your class. ;)

- I hope everything goes well on your trip. As I mentioned before, my best wishes to you and your family. Your wife is very nice, and I would like to thank you both for the "The Most Conscientious Award" and for the In-N-Out certificate. All that attention means a lot to me. I don't have enough words to express my appreciation for your generosity. Thank you again and have a wonderful Christmas.

- I just wanted to tell you "thank you" for all of the awards that you gave to us. I was truly honored by all of them, especially the MVS [Most Valuable Student] one. Thank you so much. That really meant a lot to me. Your wife is a really nice woman, and I am thankful that she was able to be there in your absence. It is so good to see that you have such a great relationship that has lasted so long. It is very encouraging to me as I will be proposing to my girlfriend later this month. Thanks for modeling so many great things to this class. That is so nice of you to go out of your way and to spend that kind of money on us with those gift certificates to In-N-Out Burger. I can't wait; I love that place!

- I will look forward to purchasing your next book. When do you expect it to come out, and/or is it okay for me to e-mail you later on? Thanks for all your knowledge and expertise to help us with our career. You've been such an excellent coach!

- Dear Professor Uda, I thank you for your encouragement all semester long. I truly feel I have gained an advantage over my peers in obtaining a great job!

- You truly are a great professor and stand out from the rest. You are passionate and energetic about what you teach, and that is what makes your class what it is. I am thankful that I took your class because not only did I learn a lot from you during the semester, but I still am learning. Best wishes always.

- Dear Professor Uda: I just wanted to send you a quick note to thank you for all of the lessons you taught me within your class. I learned a lot, which has helped me in implementing a successful job search. I am currently interviewing with many companies, and I believe that it was your help with my resume that got my foot in the door. Also, I am definitely using my SAR stories. I am interviewing with a company on Wednesday that requires five "pre-packaged stories" (i.e., SAR stories) for my next interview. Once again, thank you for all of your help, and I will keep you posted!

About the Author

Robert T. "Bob" Uda was born and raised in Hawaii for 20 years. He is the third of seven children of Masao and Irene Kuualoha Uda (both deceased). In the 40 years since leaving Hawaii, he has lived in Oklahoma, Ohio, Florida, Connecticut, and California with short stints in Utah, Alabama, Massachusetts, Texas, and Washington. He has traveled in 46 of our 50 states as well as in Canada and Mexico.

Bob earned BS degrees in aerospace engineering from the University of Oklahoma and in general business from Regents College of the University of the State of New York (now called Excelsior College). He further earned an MS degree in astronautics from the Air Force Institute of Technology and an MBA degree from the University of La Verne located in La Verne, California. Furthermore, he received a diploma in The Executive Program in Management from the UCLA Graduate School of Management.

Bob currently serves as professor of systems acquisition management at the Defense Acquisition University (DAU) where he teaches program management. He serves as a member of the Board of Regents (BOR) of the Institute of Certified Professional Managers (ICPM). Furthermore, he serves as director and vice president of the International Technology Institute (ITI).

In the USAF, he served as officer career manager of the Space and Missile Systems Organization (SAMSO), now called Space and Missile Systems Center (SMC). He held over 2,000 career counseling sessions with Air Force officers in the SAMSO on assignments, education and training, career broadening, and other personnel matters.

An award-winning writer, Bob has prepared over 35 publications including 10 books, five of them related to career development (including this book). One of these books is titled *Career Quest for College Graduates: Developing a Successful Career by Leveraging Each of Your Jobs*. A second book is titled *Career Quest for College Students: Career Development for Those Who Plan to Have a Successful Career*. A third book is titled *Resumes That Pack a Punch! Creating Beefy Bullets That Grab, Hook, and Wow Hiring Managers into Calling You for an Interview*. Additionally, a fourth book is titled *What Hue is Your Bungee Cord? Job Searching Strategies for Those Over 40 Years of Age*.

He taught logistics management courses to graduate students as an adjunct faculty member of National University. As a career coach with Bob Uda and Associates, he taught undergraduate students in "Career Development" at California State University San Marcos. He also taught "Writing and Publishing" with the Cal State San Marcos Extended Studies Office.

He is a fellow in the British Interplanetary Society, associate fellow in the American Institute of Aeronautics and Astronautics, executive member of the Academy of Management, Certified Manager (CM) with the Institute of Certified Professional Managers, and a founding charter member of the Association of Proposal Management Professionals.

Internationally recognized, he is listed in 46 Who's Who publications including *Who's Who in the World*, *Who's Who in America*, *Who's Who in California*, and *Who's Who in Science and Engineering*. He was the District 12 Write-up Winner as well as the State Write-up Winner in the California Jaycees.

Along with co-authors Dr. Istvan Tuba and Dr. Anthony Etele, Bob received a Certificate of Excellence as a finalist in the Best Published Non-fiction Books of 2005, Politics and Social Science category, with their book titled *The Third Resource: A Universal Ideology of Economics* at The 12th Annual San Diego Book Awards sponsored by the San Diego Book Awards Association, Inc., on May 20, 2006.

Bob and his wife, the former Karen Elizabeth Rowland of Circleville, Ohio, sired two sons, a daughter, and four grandchildren. You can contact Bob Uda by emailing him at bobuda@adelphia.net.

Index

978-0-595-40249-6
0-595-40249-6

www.ingramcontent.com/pod-product-compliance
Lightning Source LLC
Chambersburg PA
CBHW030935180526
45163CB00002B/579